Strategic Education Research Partnership

Committee on a Strategic Education Research Partnership

M.S. Donovan, A.K. Wigdor, and C.E. Snow, editors

Division of Behavioral and Social Sciences and Education

NATIONAL RESEARCH COUNCIL
OF THE NATIONAL ACADEMIES

THE NATIONAL ACADEMIES PRESS
Washington, D.C.
www.nap.edu

THE NATIONAL ACADEMIES PRESS
500 Fifth Street, N.W. • Washington, DC 20001

NOTICE: The project that is the subject of this report was approved by the Governing Board of the National Research Council, whose members are drawn from the councils of the National Academy of Sciences, the National Academy of Engineering, and the Institute of Medicine. The members of the committee responsible for the report were chosen for their special competences and with regard for appropriate balance.

This study was supported by Grant No. R305U000002 between the National Academy of Sciences and the U.S. Department of Education; Grant No. 00-61980-HCD from the John D. and Catherine T. MacArthur Foundation; Grant Nos. 200200171 and 20030091 from the Spencer Foundation; and Grant No. B7070 from Carnegie Corporation of New York. Any opinions, findings, conclusions, or recommendations expressed in this publication are those of the author(s) and do not necessarily reflect the views of the organizations or agencies that provided support for the project.

Library of Congress Cataloging-in-Publication Data
National Research Council (U.S.). Committee on a Strategic Education Research Partnership.
    Strategic education research partnership / Committee on a Strategic Education Research Partnership ; M.S. Donovan, A.K. Wigdor, and C.E. Snow, editors.
       p. cm.
"Division of Behavioral and Social Sciences and Education."
    ISBN 0-309-08879-8 (pbk.) — ISBN 0-309-50727-8 (PDF)
    1. Education—Research—United States. 2. School improvement programs—United States. I. Donovan, Suzanne. II. Wigdor, Alexandra K. III. Snow, Catherine E. IV. Title.
    LB1028.25.U6N37 2003
    370'.7'2—dc21

                             2003008695

Additional copies of this report are available from the National Academies Press, 500 Fifth Street, N.W., Lockbox 285, Washington, DC 20055; (800) 624-6242 or (202) 334-3313 (in the Washington metropolitan area); Internet, http://www.nap.edu

Printed in the United States of America.

Suggested citation: National Research Council. (2003). *Strategic Education Research Partnership*. Committee on a Strategic Education Research Partnership. M.S. Donovan, A.K. Wigdor, and C.E. Snow, editors. Division of Behavioral and Social Sciences and Education. Washington, DC: The National Academies Press.

THE NATIONAL ACADEMIES
Advisers to the Nation on Science, Engineering, and Medicine

The **National Academy of Sciences** is a private, nonprofit, self-perpetuating society of distinguished scholars engaged in scientific and engineering research, dedicated to the furtherance of science and technology and to their use for the general welfare. Upon the authority of the charter granted to it by the Congress in 1863, the Academy has a mandate that requires it to advise the federal government on scientific and technical matters. Dr. Bruce M. Alberts is president of the National Academy of Sciences.

The **National Academy of Engineering** was established in 1964, under the charter of the National Academy of Sciences, as a parallel organization of outstanding engineers. It is autonomous in its administration and in the selection of its members, sharing with the National Academy of Sciences the responsibility for advising the federal government. The National Academy of Engineering also sponsors engineering programs aimed at meeting national needs, encourages education and research, and recognizes the superior achievements of engineers. Dr. Wm. A. Wulf is president of the National Academy of Engineering.

The **Institute of Medicine** was established in 1970 by the National Academy of Sciences to secure the services of eminent members of appropriate professions in the examination of policy matters pertaining to the health of the public. The Institute acts under the responsibility given to the National Academy of Sciences by its congressional charter to be an adviser to the federal government and, upon its own initiative, to identify issues of medical care, research, and education. Dr. Harvey V. Fineberg is president of the Institute of Medicine.

The **National Research Council** was organized by the National Academy of Sciences in 1916 to associate the broad community of science and technology with the Academy's purposes of furthering knowledge and advising the federal government. Functioning in accordance with general policies determined by the Academy, the Council has become the principal operating agency of both the National Academy of Sciences and the National Academy of Engineering in providing services to the government, the public, and the scientific and engineering communities. The Council is administered jointly by both Academies and the Institute of Medicine. Dr. Bruce M. Alberts and Dr. Wm. A. Wulf are chair and vice chair, respectively, of the National Research Council.

www.national-academies.org

PANEL ON LEARNING AND INSTRUCTION
STRATEGIC EDUCATION RESEARCH PARTNERSHIP

Acknowledgments

The committee is grateful to the many people who contributed to this phase in the development of a Strategic Education Research Partnership (SERP). The financial support of our sponsors at the Department of Education, the John D. and Catherine T. MacArthur Foundation, Carnegie Corporation of New York, and the Spencer Foundation was essential, of course, but representatives of each also participated in fruitful discussions with the committee. Our thanks to C. Kent McGuire, former assistant secretary of education research and improvement and to his successor and now director of the National Institute for Education Sciences, Grover J. Russ Whitehurst; thanks likewise are due to Valerie Reyna, Mark Constas, and Sue Betka. We are grateful to Daniel Fallon, director of the education program at Carnegie Corporation, his predecessor Vivien Stewart, and colleague Karin Egan; Ellen Condliffe Lagemann, president of the Spencer Foundation, and Paul Goren, vice president of the Spencer Foundation and before that education officer at the MacArthur Foundation.

In the course of our work, the committee drew on the expertise of many others. James A. Kelly, president of the National Board for Professional Teaching Standards, served as senior adviser to the committee throughout. Kelly is one of the few people in the country to build a new research-based program, national in scope, that has made teachers and school administrators central players in education reform. David A. Goslin, former president of the American Institutes for Research, was a vital link between the first SERP committee and this one, generously providing project memory so that the Phase 2 effort could build fruitfully on what had gone before. In thinking about the conditions required for a powerful research program, the committee benefited greatly from Emerson Elliott's deep experience and wisdom. A long-time federal career employee, Elliott occupied positions from 1957 to 2000 that placed him in the center of the federal education research enterprise, including four stints as acting director of the research function and appointment as the first commissioner of education statistics in 1992. His paper, commissioned by the committee and entitled *Three Visions for Investment in Education Research: An Insider's Recollections from Four Decades in Federal Policy and Practice* (January 2002) appears in condensed form as Appendix A.

The committee extends its appreciation to participants in a workshop on the organization of research and its relation to practice in other sectors, held in November 2000. Richard Klausner, then director of the National Cancer Institute, and Annetine C. Gelijns and Alan J. Moskowitz, codirectors of the International Center for Health Outcomes and Innovation Research, Columbia University, gave us insight into important aspects of the medical sector. Internationally known agricultural economists Vernon Ruttan of the University of Minnesota and Robert E. Evenson of Yale University shared their knowledge of the system linking research, product development, and farming through federal and state programs (the agricultural experiment stations, the extension service) and, more recently, through private-sector investment. In addition, the committee benefited from papers commissioned from Linda Argoty of Carnegie Mellon University and James Rosenbaum of Northwestern University on organizational research and educational change.

The committee's work was enhanced by the Panel on Learning and Instruction, whose chair, James Pellegrino, attended all committee meetings to ensure adequate communication and coordination between committee and panel. The panel's report, *Learning and Instruction: A SERP Research Agenda*, is being published as a companion volume to this report.

A special note of thanks is due to committee members Catherine Snow and John Reed, who agreed to take on the role of vice chair to help us accomplish a great deal of work in all-too-little time.

Our thanks go as well to Timothy Ready, who helped get things started, to administrative assistants Shirley Thatcher and Allison Shoup, and to Kirsten Sampson Snyder, who managed the review process.

This report has been reviewed in draft form by individuals

chosen for their diverse perspectives and technical expertise, in accordance with procedures approved by the Report Review Committee of the National Research Council. The purpose of this independent review is to provide candid and critical comments that will assist the institution in making its published report as sound as possible and to ensure that the report meets institutional standards for objectivity, evidence, and responsiveness to the study charge. The review comments and draft manuscript remain confidential to protect the integrity of the deliberative process.

We wish to thank the following individuals for their review of this report: Sherri Andrews, General Studies, North Carolina School of the Arts, Winston-Salem, NC; Nicholas A. Branca, Mathematical and Computer Sciences, San Diego State University; James R. Brown, Superintendent, Glendale Unified School District, CA; Anthony S. Bryk, Center for School Improvement, The University of Chicago; Williamson M. Evers, Hoover Institution, Stanford University; Richard M. Felder, Department of Chemical Engineering, North Carolina State University; Henry M. Levin, Teachers College, Columbia University; Marcia C. Linn, Graduate School of Education, University of California, Berkeley; James G. March, Graduate School of Business–Dean's Office, Stanford University; Lorraine McDonnell, Department of Political Science, University of California, Santa Barbara; Barbara Schneider, Sociology and Human Development, The University of Chicago; and Neil J. Smelser, Department of Sociology, University of California, Berkeley.

Although the reviewers listed above have provided many constructive comments and suggestions, they were not asked to endorse the conclusions or recommendations nor did they see the final draft of the report before its release. The review of this report was overseen by William Danforth, Washington University, St. Louis, and Richard Shavelson, School of Education, Stanford University. Appointed by the National Research Council, they were responsible for making certain that an independent examination of this report was carried out in accordance with institutional procedures and that all review comments were carefully considered. Responsibility for the final content of this report rests entirely with the authoring committee and the institution.

In addition to the NRC-led review, the committee invited external review from four others, to whom we extend our thanks:

Chester Finn, senior fellow at the Hoover Institution and president of the Thomas B. Fordham Foundation; Steven Fleischman, executive director of the Education Quality Institute; James Guthrie, director of the Peabody Center for Education Policy at Vanderbilt University; and Mary Anne Schmitt, president of the New American Schools.

Joe B. Wyatt, *Chair*
Alexandra K. Wigdor, *Director*
Committee on the Strategic
Education Research Partnership

Contents

Foreword

I n 1996, the National Research Council, the working arm of the National Academy of Sciences and its sister institutions (henceforth, the National Academies), established a committee composed of educators, researchers, and policy experts to examine whether it might be feasible to mount a strategic program of education research that could make a strong contribution to improving education in the United States. Their answer, somewhat to the surprise of the committee members, turned out to be a unanimous and enthusiastic "yes!"

The committee's report was published in 1999. Entitled *Improving Student Learning: A Strategic Plan for Education Research and Its Utilization*, it proposed—as an ambitious experiment—the establishment of a new research program focused on obtaining answers to four specific questions:

- **How can advances in research on human cognition, development, and learning be incorporated into educational practice?**
- **How can student engagement in the learning process and motivation to achieve in school be increased?**
- **How can schools and school districts be transformed into organizations that have the capacity to continuously improve their practices?**
- **How can the use of research knowledge be increased in schools and school districts?**

To address the above questions, the committee called for a large-scale program of research, development, and evaluation. Its report pointed out that much of the work would need to be embedded in school settings, and that it should be informed by the needs of the most challenging schools—in particular, high-poverty urban schools. Proposing a "built-in partnership" of research, policy, and practice, the report recommended that the new research program be "focused, collaborative, cumulative, sustained, and solutions oriented."

With generous support from the U.S. Department of Education, the MacArthur Foundation, Carnegie Corporation of New York, and the Spencer Foundation, the National Academies have been able to build on the powerful vision presented in *Improving Student Learning* with this follow-up report. A new committee, convened in early 2001, was charged with the task of elaborating and refining—both organizationally and substantively—the general plan outlined in the first report. To enable it to deal with organizational design issues, the new committee included not only education practitioners and researchers, but also those who either have served as leaders of successful organizations or have studied them.

The committee's report that follows lays out, in considerable detail, a proposal for a Strategic Education Research Partnership (SERP). Representing a call to action, it focuses on generating a much more vigorous connection between research and the practice of education. Among its most important and novel elements is the conclusion that the states should become both the major clients and the supporters of a long-term, sustained effort dedicated to applying the best possible science to the process of educational improvement. Critical to the success of the partnership will be the generation of a new spirit of sharing and cooperation between education researchers, as emphasized throughout the report. How might such a goal be achieved?

An experience from a different area of research is relevant here. I began my own work in science policy in 1986, when I was asked to chair a committee of the National Academies that would examine whether there should be a major project in the United States to map and sequence the human genome. My committee was initially quite divided on this issue. But we quickly reached the conclusion that a special project was indeed essential. One of the decisive factors in our decision was the belief that we could enforce a new culture of sharing among scientists in the field of human genetics by enforcing the appropriate standards through a special funding mechanism.

And so it turned out. As I write this foreword, the finished sequence of the human genome is about to be published, following the plan that was laid out in the National Academies report 15 years earlier. This remarkable achievement was possible only because of the intense teamwork exhibited by all those who participated in the publicly funded Human Genome Project. The aims of a SERP are certainly no less critical to our future than those of improving our health through biomedical research. Thus, in principle, the research program envisioned in this report should generate the same type of excitement, sense of public service, and widespread support as did our 1988 report *Mapping and Sequencing the Human Genome*.

In order to further dissect the process of making research useful to teachers, school administrators, and policy officials, a special expert Panel on Learning and Instruction was established to pursue the first question posed in *Improving Student Learning*. Its membership includes teachers, cognitive and developmental scientists, and subject matter specialists—all of whom have been engaged with the problems of practice. Chapter 4 of this report is drawn from that panel's work. And the full product of their deliberations is presented in the companion volume, *Learning and Instruction: A SERP Research Agenda*.

We look forward to the end of SERP as an initiative of the National Academies and the *beginning* of its life as a joint venture of partners who are committed to improving student learning in the United States. The National Academies recognize the critical importance of improving the education of our nation's young; we therefore stand ready to serve as part of the broad coalition that will be needed to launch this endeavor successfully in the years ahead.

Bruce Alberts
President, National Academy of Sciences
Chair, National Research Council

Executive Summary

Envision a cadre of leading scientists and practitioners working together on a coherent, highly focused program of education research that is tightly coupled and interactive with practice. They are guided and supported by the kind of organizational infrastructure needed to plan, manage, and carry out a sustained program of research and development. They work in collaborative teams, and much of the research is carried out in school settings around the country. As the research teams learn over time how to cultivate the substance and processes of research-based practice, they come to embody a new model of practitioners and researchers familiar with and comfortable in both the world of research and of practice.

The Strategic Education Research Partnership (SERP) proposed here is designed to make this vision a reality. It has several distinct dimensions. *First, SERP is a program of "use-inspired" research and development.* This means that problems of practice will be at center stage in determining the research and development agenda; the program will place as much emphasis on follow-through to link knowledge and products as on theoretical grounding. *Second, SERP is an organization,* designed to provide the infrastructure to make a coherent, sustained research, development, and implementation program possible. *And third, SERP is a partnership* between the research and practice communities, and among the communities that will need to join together to support the creation and maintenance of the SERP enterprise.

THE NEED

There have been many programs of educational research supported by federal agencies and private foundations designed to improve student outcomes. They have generated important research-based knowledge, but their efforts have not effectively penetrated educational practice. Education does not presently function like medicine or agriculture, where close linkages between research and practice have had major influences on both.

Three sets of powerful but underutilized resources convince us that a SERP research and development enterprise could support genuine improvements in student achievement: (1) advances in the disciplines with relevance to education (cognitive science, developmental psychology, organizational theory) that are largely untapped; (2) natural variations in educational practice that have not been studied systematically; and, (3) innovations in educational practice and policy that have been demonstrated to be effective, at least in particular settings, but have not been sufficiently developed or studied for purposes of moving to scale so that they have broad influence on student outcomes.

The problem of effectively capitalizing on these resources poses several challenges:

- There is currently no institution in which education practitioners and researchers from a variety of disciplines are provided with support to interact, collaborate, and learn from each other. Thus, researchers often fail to bring important understandings to the stage of usability, and practitioners have no way either to analyze and systematize their own wisdom of practice or to influence the directions and shape of the research agenda. Moreover, researchers have little opportunity to see and try to understand the variety of practices and outcomes that characterize the operational setting.

- There are too few resources and too little stability in funding to support the development and evaluation of promising innovations in teaching, curriculum, and assessment, so even the best innovations frequently are not carried beyond initial demonstrations of effectiveness.

- There is no site where a carefully vetted knowledge base about instructional innovation, school reform, and education policy resides and accumulates.
- There are few vehicles for conceptually coherent research planning so that research agendas tend to resemble topical lists responsive to neither the strengths of research nor the complexities of practice.

· ·

THE GOAL

The Strategic Education Research Partnership is designed to reshape the education research and development landscape to meet these challenges:

SERP will seek to forge a new kind of partnership among researchers, practitioners, and policy makers, generating collaborative work that will in turn help develop new capabilities among researchers and educators. This means that SERP needs to be a place where researchers, policy makers, and practitioners can work collaboratively, where the ethos is one of respect for the many kinds of knowledge and experience needed to advance research-based educational practice.

SERP will seek to build a coherent research program with well-justified priorities. There must be organizational mechanisms for coordinated agenda setting, frequent stock taking, and a conscious process of iterative knowledge building. The development of common research protocols and data systems will also promote coherence and responsiveness to the needs of practice and policy.

SERP will seek to ensure high standards and rigorous attention to methodological excellence. There must be a deep institutional commitment to quality assurance and review processes, expressed both in appropriate oversight mechanisms and in a culture of rigor and excellence that infuses the entire enterprise.

SERP will take research into field settings so that innovations can be introduced, analyzed, developed, and evaluated. Equally important, researchers will be able to study what is going on in actual practice. The organizational capacity to gain and support access to clinical research settings—schools, school districts, teacher education programs—is critical. By lowering the formidable transaction costs for researchers and schools of establishing a working partnership, the use-inspired orientation and collaborative relationships that characterize the SERP vision become far more attainable.

SERP will seek to attract first-rate scientists and practitioners to work in and with the field sites by creating conditions for the induction of new members into the collaborative work and facilitating expanded career opportunities for both the researchers and practitioners who commit to the SERP use-inspired research and development. A major incentive for researchers and reflective practitioners will be the availability of high-quality data, and the reduced transaction costs of carrying out research in school settings.

SERP will promote access to and use of the information and innovations it generates. This will require organizational commitment to accumulating and making sense of findings, careful screening for scientific quality, and the investigation of effective mechanisms for communication and the development of multiple presentations of knowledge for different audiences.

Finally, to function effectively, *the SERP enterprise will require a supporting infrastructure* that provides the security of an extended time frame and stability across periods of political change, as well as a great deal more money than has traditionally been devoted to educational research. The initial amount must be sufficient to provide for the effective incubation of a new research and development system for education.

THE SERP DESIGN

The structure envisioned for SERP has three basic components: (1) a central organization or headquarters responsible for program design and coherence, quality control, communications, financial oversight, and long-term planning, where an internal research program is also located; (2) distributed research and development teams that muster the nation's expertise to the enterprise; and (3) a set of field sites—school districts or groups of districts where practitioners and researchers work together to define and pursue key questions and puzzles regarding practice and lines of development and implementation research. All of these—headquarters, research teams, and field sites—will make common cause in a series of collaborative research and development networks.

We propose three initial networks that we believe are critical to the SERP mission. The first is a learning and instruction network, which would build its agenda from the problems of classroom practice and approach its research and development through the lenses of the cognitive and psychological sciences. The second network, closely tied to the first, is on schools as organizations. It would build its agenda from the problems of creating organizational environments and incentives that encourage organizational learning and support productive changes in instruction. Its research will draw on sociology and organizational theory to help schools and school systems become more effective. The third network would focus on education policy. Its agenda would respond to the needs of policy makers to better understand the outcomes and consequences of such policy decisions as class- and school-size changes, accountability standards, school governance changes, and education finance arrangements. Much of its work would draw on the economic and political sciences.

The proposed SERP networks would provide the physical link between schools and school districts, on one hand, and the research community, on the other. This partnership in a common and carefully planned enterprise is what will make possible the key innovative characteristics of the SERP endeavor:

- Placement of the problems of practice at center stage in determining the research agenda;
- Exploitation of many sources of knowledge, including behavioral and social science research, subject-matter scholarship, and, not least, effective practice;
- Systematic linkage among elements that are typically treated separately in educational research—student learning, teacher learning, the organizational context of schooling, and education policy;
- Development of mechanisms that accumulate knowledge dynamically;
- Rigorous attention to replication and the systematic building of scientific knowledge;
- The construction of a detailed, longitudinal database; and
- Conceptualizing student, teacher, and organizational learning as long-term developmental processes.

LAUNCHING SERP

This report is addressed to state and federal policy makers, educators and administrators, the research and university communities, and private foundations and businesses. It is a call to mobilize the nation's resources and political will, the power of scientific research, and the expertise of those who educate the nation's children through a Strategic Education Research Partnership.

Linking research to education practice effectively will require the commitment of those who are ultimately responsible for the form that practice takes. There are, clearly, many stakeholders for whom education issues are a high priority, but none with greater authority over, or responsibility for, student outcomes than state policy makers. Therefore, we recommend that a compact of state governments be formed for the purposes of collectively advancing the knowledge base and instructional resources to support their single largest commitment: the provision of education. Although states have not historically played a major role in education research and development, the logic for that role is sound: the size and continuity of an investment in research and development should reflect the return it offers in the form of improved service delivery and lower costs in the long run (e.g., grade repetition and special education). Nevertheless, we do not propose SERP as a state activity alone. To promote change of the magnitude we propose here will require building a broad coalition of powerful partners. That coalition might include Congress, federal agencies, and private foundations and businesses.

To demonstrate the benefits of a research and development investment of this kind will require funding during a launch and start-up period. The costs of start-up will vary enormously depending on the assumptions about the pace of launch and the number and size of individual projects. Under the assumption that capacity to do the kind of work envisioned will have to be built during the first decade, as will the commitment of resources, we anticipate a relatively conservative program size and pace of expansion during the start-up years. An illustrative set of estimates commissioned by the committee put start-up costs in the neighborhood of $500 million over seven years.

Launch activities in the first two years would cost relatively little. Costs would build in the later years, as the research projects increase in number and scope. Ultimately, a SERP enterprise capable of carrying out the broad mission envisioned here will require a considerably larger investment. While the size of the investment envisioned may be daunting given the meager funds traditionally allocated for education R&D and current fiscal strains, even 0.5 to 1 percent of the budget for elementary and secondary education would yield two to four times the amount estimated for the first seven years. For any sector of the economy, this is a relatively small rate of investment in research and development.

Negotiating funding for a proof-of-concept period of 7 to 10 years is, in our judgment, a prerequisite for success. Because of their greater flexibility, we call on private foundations to take the lead in funding in the early years. This is a leadership role that major foundations have taken on at critical junctures in the past. Additional substantial backing might be sought from businesses, the U.S. Congress, and federal agencies during the launch stage. We propose that states not incur a financial obligation when they join the compact, but that they commit to contributing a small portion (a fraction of 1 percent) of their K-12 spending further down the road, so that political commitment will grow to embrace financial obligation.

How much of that investment will be new, and how much can come from available resource pools, or from redirecting resources currently allocated to activities that can be carried out as part of the SERP effort, will be determined as SERP unfolds. For example, resources through Title I and through the No Child Left Behind Act of 2001 support research-based practice, evaluation of practice, and data collection and evaluation. Just as we propose SERP as an effort to build on, and make more of, existing research and development efforts, start-up efforts can also build from existing resources that states may be able to use more effectively utilized in the SERP organizational context.

With this report SERP ends as a National Academies activity and begins a new chapter. Conceived and nurtured as an initiative of the National Academies, its future success now must hinge on the will and resources of a broad coalition of partners committed to improving student learning in the United

States. The National Academies recognize the critical importance of improving education in this nation and therefore stand
ready to support the partners in SERP as they move forward to
shape the SERP agenda and implement the bold ideas set forth
in this report.

1 The Need for a New Partnership

THE CHALLENGE

A powerful consensus has emerged in the United States about the importance of improving student learning, particularly for children in elementary and secondary schools. This consensus has led to significant federal and state investment in education. To make that investment productive, however, will require a commensurate effort to investigate systematically *how* to improve teaching and learning. A proliferation of content and accountability standards has not been accompanied by companion efforts to ascertain whether and how those standards can be reached for the highly diverse population of students to whom they apply. It is perplexing that so high a national priority has to date generated so little sustained, systematic attention to the very complex problems of teaching and learning in the classroom, and has fostered so little fruitful collaboration among researchers, education practitioners, and policy makers.

The current state of affairs cannot, in our view, be attributed simply to a lack of attention by researchers to problems that bear on student learning or to a shortage of intellectual paradigms that might profitably be applied. There are powerful examples of both. Nor can it be attributed to a lack of intriguing experiments in the communities of educational practice that provide fodder for research. Efforts at innovation and reform abound. Rather, the existing pockets of opportunity created by research and experimentation have been largely untapped. The committee's judgment is that there are two explanations for this: first, historically there have been few incentives for change in education, and second, there are no institutions within which collaborative efforts to improve student learning are facilitated.

The links between research and practice, between scientists and educators, are tenuous and fragile.

A change in incentives is on the horizon. State and federal policies focused on establishing standards and measuring student performance place new demands on schools to improve student learning. In response, policy makers and school officials are beginning to actively seek the sort of research and development that would help schools improve performance outcomes. But the structures that would respond effectively to that demand are largely absent. The question therefore is "How do we construct a focused program of research and development that informs and improves day-to-day educational practice?"

In our view, the answer lies not in more of the same but in a fundamentally different model for education research and development. The centerpiece of this new model is collaboration between practitioners and researchers, enabled and supported by a new organizational infrastructure. We propose the Strategic Education Research Partnership (SERP) as that new model. At the core of the SERP vision are teams of leading scientists and practitioners working together on a coherent, highly focused program of research and development that is tightly coupled and interactive with practice. Building on behavioral and social science research, disciplinary research, and the systematic study of effective practice, their efforts can produce, over time, a powerful body of usable knowledge.

But this will happen only if SERP, through its organization and program, develops and nurtures the capacity for the work that is envisioned. A critical element of the SERP plan, then, is to cultivate practitioners who have the knowledge and training needed to work effectively with research teams, helping to develop, test, and use research-based materials and methods; researchers who focus their work on the problems of educational practice as they develop and test hypotheses in collaboration with classroom teachers; and developers who have learned how to work with practitioners and researchers to incorporate robust findings into usable, carefully tested instructional methods, programs and tools, organizational environments, and professional development programs. To achieve this end, the SERP organization must foster the development of the shared language, mutual regard, and working atmosphere *required* for effective partnering.

Equally important, the collaboration we envision extends beyond the SERP research activities. As the research accumulates, the same intense collaborative effort must go into synthesis, sense-making, and communication, so that SERP can become a place where teachers and school administrators, policy officials, schools of education, researchers, and other participants in the education enterprise can go for high-quality, carefully evaluated research-based information; a place where interested school districts and researchers can link up around the SERP agenda; a place where new members of the field of teaching and its related research disciplines can join a program of research and development productively channeled to improving teaching and learning (we will propose fellowship and internship programs); and a place where many kinds of funders of education research and development can become part of an ongoing collaborative effort to improve student outcomes.

UNTAPPED RESOURCES

Would a new research and development infrastructure improve educational outcomes? The committee's optimism about the potential to do so is rooted in three sets of untapped resources that could make this new kind of research enterprise highly productive.

First, there are tantalizing opportunities to leverage intellectual developments in allied fields and disciplines in pursuit of improved educational outcomes. The outpouring of scientific discovery on the mind and brain, on the processes of thinking and learning, on the neural underpinnings of learning and cognition, and on the development of intellectual competencies provide a rich context for innovation in education (National Research Council, 1999, 2000). The enthusiastic response to the National Research Council report, *How People Learn: Brain, Mind, Experience, and School*, suggests a growing interest in that research base and its relevance for teaching and learning.

Second, remarkable "natural experiments" in educational practice are occurring every day. Yet for the most part these have not been the object of systematic, rigorous, sustained study and evaluation by researchers. These natural experiments range from the work of individual teachers who have consistent records of supporting high student achievement, to schools and school districts that undertake reform efforts, to new forms of organization like charter schools. But while prescriptions for educational reform are numerous, there are relatively few careful research efforts designed to evaluate how and why differences in the form and content of education affect student learning.

Third, and perhaps most distressing, there are numerous examples of promising educational innovations that have been validated through rigorous research but that have had relatively little impact on educational practice. The Number Worlds curriculum, for example, was designed to build on years of

• •

BOX 1.1 Primary School Mathematics

From an early age, children begin to develop an informal understanding of quantity and number. Careful research conducted by developmental and cognitive psychologists has mapped the progression of children's conceptual understanding of number through the preschool years. Just as healthy children who live in language-rich environments will develop the ability to speak according to a fairly typical trajectory (from single sound utterances to grammatically correct explanations of why a parent should not turn out the light and leave at bedtime), children follow a fairly typical trajectory from differentiating more from less, to possessing the facility to add and subtract accurately with small numbers. Just as a child's environment influences language development, it influences the acquisition of number concepts. For many children whose early years are characterized by disadvantage, there is a substantial lag in the development of the number concepts that are prerequisite to first grade mathematics.

Between the ages of 4 and 6 most children develop what Case and Sandieson (1987) refer to as the "central conceptual structure" for whole number mathematics:

1. The ability to verbally count using number words. This ability is initially developed as a sequencing of words (one, two, three. . .) without an understanding of the specific meaning attached to the words. Quantity is still understood nonnumerically as more or less, big or small.
2. The ability to count with one to one correspondence. When this ability develops, children are able to point at objects as they count, mapping the counting words onto the objects so that each is tagged once and only once. This ability is initially developed as a sensorimotor activity, with an understanding of *quantity* still absent. Children who can successfully count four objects and five objects cannot answer the question, "Which is more, four or five?"
3. The ability to recognize quantity as set size. With development of this ability, children do understand that "three" refers to a set with three members. Initially this understanding is concrete, and children will often use their fingers as indicators of set membership.
4. The ability to "mentally simulate" the sensorimotor counting. When this ability is in place, children can carry out counting tasks as though they were operating with a mental number line. They understand that movement from one set size to the next involves the addition or subtraction of one unit.

Children from middle and higher socioeconomic backgrounds generally come to school with the central conceptual structure in place, whereas many children from disadvantaged backgrounds do not. When first grade math instruction assumes that knowledge, these children are less likely to succeed.

A curriculum called Number Worlds deliberately puts the central conceptual structure for whole numbers in place in kindergarten (Griffin and Case, 1997). Developed, tested, and refined with classroom teachers and children, the program consists primarily of 78 games that provide children with ample opportunity for hands-on, inquiry-based learning. Number is represented in a variety of forms—on dice, with chips, as spaces on a board, as written numerals. An important component of the program is the Number Knowledge Test, which allows teachers to quickly assess each individual student's current level of understanding and then choose individual or class activities that will solidify fragile knowledge and take students the next step.

careful research on children's understanding of whole number (see Box 1.1). The experimental results suggest that disadvantaged children who begin school as much as two years behind their peers in number knowledge can be brought up to—and in some cases surpass—the level of those peers in the early elementary years. Other innovations in instruction (e.g., Reciprocal Teaching, Thinker Tools), in professional development (e.g., Cognitively Guided Instruction) and in aspects of school organization (e.g., reduced class size, small schools) have demon-

• •

The Number Worlds program has been tested with disadvantaged populations in numerous controlled trials in both the United States and Canada with positive results. One longitudinal study charted the progress of three groups of children attending school in an urban community in Massachusetts for three years: from the beginning of kindergarten to the end of second grade. Children in both the Number Worlds treatment group (n = 54) and in the control group (n = 48) were from schools in low-income, high-risk communities where about 79 percent of children were eligible for free or reduced-price lunch. A third normative group (n = 78) was drawn from a magnet school in the urban center that had attracted a large number of majority students. The student body was predominantly middle income, with 37 percent eligible for free or reduced-price lunch.

The Number Knowledge Test scores on the vertical axis can be mapped against developmental expectations for children at various ages (at age 6, the expected developmental score is 1.0, at 7 it is 1.5, and at 8 it is 2.0). As Figure 1.1 shows, the normative group began kindergarten with substantially higher scores on the Number Knowledge Test than children in the treatment and the control groups. The gap indicated a developmental lag that exceeded one year and was closer to two years for many children in the treatment group. By the end of the kindergarten year, however, the Number Worlds children narrowed the gap with the normative group to a small fraction of its initial size. By the end of the second grade, the treatment children actually outperformed the magnet school group. In contrast, the initial gap between the control group children and the normative group did not narrow over time. The control group children did make steady progress over the three years; however, they were never able to catch up.

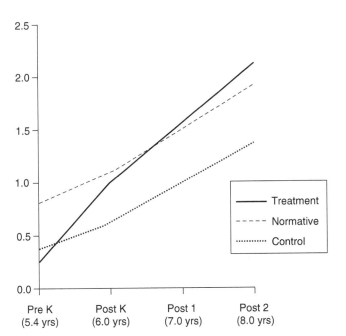

FIGURE 1.1 Mean developmental level scores on Number Knowledge Test at four time periods (SOURCE: Case et al., 1999).

strable strengths.[1] Some of these have been based on careful research into learning and teaching (Palincsar, 1986; Palincsar and Herrenkohl, 2002; White and Frederiksen, 1998) and have benefited from being implemented in situations where practitioners could modify their design and enhance their utility. Many of these innovations have been demonstrated in research studies to be effective in improving learning substantially, even to weaken the customary link between performance and such factors as family income, race, and other demographic factors. Despite these successes, the innovations have not penetrated deeply into mainstream practice.

THE NEED FOR AN R&D INFRASTRUCTURE

To effectively mine untapped resources for purposes of improving education will require, in the committee's view, the development of a research and development infrastructure to that has several key functions.

Recruiting Disciplinary Scholarship

In many sectors of the economy, what is of interest to academic researchers is not the same—and may hardly intersect—with what is of interest to practitioners in that sector. Theories and paradigms of researchers may be relevant to, but not applied to, problems of practice.

This problem is not unique to education. Indeed, the inspiration for the SERP idea at the National Research Council was the Strategic Highway Research Program, launched in the 1980s to focus research efforts on the problems of highway construction. At that time, policy makers charged with the construction of a highway system and construction companies charged with building those highways did not have the knowledge base to support the construction of longer lasting roads that were customized to local environmental conditions. They were uninterested in funding research, however, because what researchers produced was, in their view, of little practical importance. The National Academy of Sciences proposed, and the U.S. Congress funded, a 10-year program of research focused on the problems of practice. The collaborative efforts of those from the worlds of

---

[1]For further discussion of these and other programs, see the companion report, *Learning and Instruction: A SERP Research Agenda.*

research, policy, and construction through the Strategic High-way Research Program were generally viewed as highly productive (National Research Council, 1999).

In other sectors as well, research and development infra-structures were designed to tackle this same issue: to bring together scientific resources and the problems of practice. Land grant colleges and agricultural experiment stations are prime examples, as are teaching hospitals in medicine. Although medicine and agriculture differ in many important respects from education,[2] the historical importance in those sectors of developing opportunities and settings to carry out a systematic program of research on practice is instructive.[3]

Access to school settings is particularly important for a program of research and development focused on educational practice because most researchers lack intimate knowledge of K-12 practice. The typical researcher's thinking about teaching, learning, or organizational change is quite different from—and much more abstract than—that of the typical teacher or administrator. Implementation, for example, tends to be seen as an issue of second-order importance. Practitioners, in contrast, spend much of their time focused on the moment, and they lack the resources or training to evaluate their own practice systematically or to share what they have learned about implementation in organizational context with colleagues. Grounding research in the problems and needs of practice will require productive relationships that are neither linear nor unidirectional; instead, research and practice must interact in meaningful and progressively more sophisticated ways.

Making educational practice the focus of serious research attention will also require access to data that are at a level of specificity that allows for an understanding of the effects of characteristics of teachers, students, instructional programs, and classroom environments on learning outcomes. These data must be collected longitudinally if the long-term impact of policies, practices, and interventions is to be understood. Longitudinal data can also play a central role in theory development, since the observation of patterns in data can stimulate hypothesis development and testing (see Box 1.2).

---

[2]Including market conditions.

[3]The committee is indebted to leading agricultural economists Vernon W. Ruttan of the University of Minnesota and Robert E. Evans of Yale University for sharing their deep knowledge of this issue.

BOX 1.2 The Amazing Miss A

A 1978 study of student achievement at the "Ray School," an elementary school located in one of the poorest areas of a large northeastern city, uncovered a startling fact: IQ can be affected by teaching. The research, conducted by Eigil Pedersen, focused on people who were pupils at the school over a 25-year period, probably beginning in the 1930s. The school had a reputation of being the most difficult among the 80 elementary schools in the district; its students consistently had the lowest mean scores on IQ tests. Only 50 percent of those who graduated from the elementary school completed tenth grade, and only 10 percent of that group completed high school.

Professor Pedersen attended the Ray School from the age of 4, and he returned there to teach fifth grade as a young teacher. Even as life took him elsewhere, he kept track of some of those who had been in his classes, becoming increasingly disheartened at how few completed high school, or even tenth grade. He ultimately came upon the idea of interviewing graduates of the Ray School to see if this might help him devise more effective teaching methods. In order to try to locate them, Pedersen reviewed the permanent record cards of pupils at the school who would now be adults. In doing so, he noticed an oddity: many pupils exhibited large differences in IQ scores between the third grade and sixth grade administrations of the tests, which went against contemporary notions of the stability of IQ.

This apparent anomaly led Pedersen and his colleagues to undertake several studies of the effects of school characteristics on IQ change, making what appears to be wonderfully clever use of the permanent records to gain estimates of such phenomena as self-esteem, self-fulfilling prophesies, and reinforcement by teachers, always with IQ score as the primary dependent variable. At some point along the way, Pedersen got curious about whether achievement in first grade is an indicator of later IQ score. Records showed that there were three first grade teachers who were at the school during the whole period under study, as well as many others who stayed for only a few years. He found that, of the long-time teachers, Miss A had taught a high proportion of the pupils who showed an increase in IQ score between third and sixth grades. Miss B had taught a high proportion of the girls whose scores increased, and Miss C had taught a high proportion of the students whose IQ scores had decreased between third and sixth grades. The students were otherwise undifferentiated by economic or other background characteristics.

Pedersen and his colleagues managed to locate 60 people in their early 30s who had attended the Ray School as children. They were interviewed in depth according to a carefully devised protocol, which yielded, among other things, a measure of "adult status," a distillation of six factors including occupation, type of housing occupied, and education. Adult status scores were then tabulated against all of the many variables in the study. "[O]ne simple tabulation was so stunning it caused them to stop and look at their data differently. . . . It was the cross tabulation of 'adult status' with first-grade teacher" (Fallon, 2001).

The mean adult status score of those who were Miss C's pupils was 4.3 in a distribution that ranged from 1.0 to 9.0. For Miss B's students it was 4.8. And for Miss A's it was 7.0. Considered on a simple scale of high, medium, and low, the adult status scores again showed dramatically differing results: for all teachers together, only 29 percent achieved high status as adults; almost 40 percent were classified as low status. None of Miss A's former students were classified as low status, and 64 percent of her students achieved high adult status although they were indistinguishable from the others in terms of background characteristics.

Fallon, speaking with and for Pedersen, emphasizes two important aspects of the study. The first was the finding that teacher quality makes a difference (against the then conventional wisdom that gains in student achievement would come from changes in poverty, socioeconomic status, and the like rather than from within the school). The second was that only a rigorous and creative use of multiple research methods enabled the authors to reach their important conclusion. Being able to link the achievement of individual students *over time* with specific teachers, curricula, and schools enabled this research to address the kinds of questions that get to the heart of the matter.

SOURCE: Distilled from Daniel Fallon, "The Amazing Miss A and Why We Should Care About Her," Homecoming Speech, University of South Carolina, October 19, 2001.

Nurturing Research
Over an Adequate Time Span

Solid research that has implications for teaching and learning exists (National Research Council, 2000). Often, however, that knowledge is not elaborated at a level of detail that is useful for practice and then incorporated into carefully tested programs and tools (directed both at student learning and at teacher learning) that allow it to infuse the larger system. A research and development infrastructure could provide an environment that nurtures promising work through the various stages needed for classroom relevance and reliability.

Sometimes research stalls at the identification of important principles of learning and teaching that are not made specific enough for practice. For example, a now substantial body of research points to the misconceptions that students harbor in physics. In making sense of everyday experience, people develop understandings, or informal models, of how the world works that shape everyday ideas about scientific relationships. These ideas usually contain partial truths but are not scientifically correct. For example, as we move closer to a heat source, temperature rises. Students often assume that the higher temperatures of the summer must mean that the earth is closer to the sun, and classroom lessons that explain the seasons in terms of the angle of the earth's axis with respect to the sun quite often fail to change that conception (Schneps and Sadler, 1987). In studies of students of all ages, everyday models of the physical world prove to be highly resistant to change (DiSessa, 1982; National Research Council, 2000, 2003b ; Vosniadou and Brewer, 1989). The difficulty of changing everyday conceptions is a phenomenon that extends into every area of the curriculum (for examples in history and mathematics, see National Research Council, 2003a). Knowing about this principle is critical to effective teaching yet it is of little help to teachers unless the work has been done to reveal the kinds of conceptions student typically harbor regarding the topic a teacher is about to tackle, as well as the teaching strategies needed for supporting conceptual change in students. A program of research focused on making the most important findings from research usable in the classroom would pursue such an agenda.

The stalling point is not always at the level of general principles, however. Many promising curricular or pedagogical innovations do not penetrate the system because individual researchers are left with the challenge of raising the funds and carrying the work forward with very little support. Reciprocal Teaching, for example, is a procedure for addressing a very pervasive problem of K-12 education—students' independent comprehension of text. The program showed impressive results, but it is not widely used. The research was not carried through to a point at which it was sufficiently embedded in curricular programs so as to be readily accessible to a large number of teachers (see Chapter 2). Number Worlds does have a well-articulated and extensive curriculum but using that curriculum effectively requires that teachers understand the teaching and learning of whole number differently. A research and development program focused on teacher knowledge and learning designed to prepare teachers to use it well has not yet been developed. The expertise and interest required for the many different tasks of research, development, evaluation, communication, and professional development are not likely to emerge from individuals working alone or even with a few colleagues. But an appropriate organizational infrastructure can knit together communities with these different strengths so that efforts can be carried through all the necessary stages for usability in the classroom.

There are other examples in which theories about learning and pedagogy are incorporated into curricula and classroom programs and tools, but research to rigorously test if, when, and for whom the programs and tools are effective is often lacking. Several National Science Foundation- (NSF) supported science and math curricula fall into this category (Education Development Center, Inc., 2001). Adequate evaluation is taken to mean not just analysis of learning outcomes, but also evidence about a program's feasibility in the classroom and its accessibility to the average teacher. It also requires attention to the perspectives of teachers trying to use the program with a wide variety of students in a variety of school settings, as well as the distribution of results across the population of students (not just evidence about average achievement outcomes).

An infrastructure that supports a major research and development program is not, of course, required in order for an evaluation to be done. What a sustained R&D program can bring to bear, however, is the capacity to assess the theoretical underpinnings of a program in order to isolate those that show particular promise for improving understanding of important issues of teaching and learning. And in proposing evaluation design and instrumentation, it can create the opportunity to learn not only if something works, but why and how. This more thoroughgoing evaluation is more likely to be the product of a research program focused on generating a deeper knowledge base regarding how students learn and teachers teach than it is to be the result of a one-shot effort to determine whether a program "works." In a program of research and development, outcomes of evaluations are a milestone but not a finish line. Both successes and failures provide clues about the mechanisms at work and the effects of context that can support new understandings and hypothesis development. Indeed, in order to understand when results can be generalized and when they cannot, knowledge of the mechanisms and of the role of context is critical.

This point applies not only to programs, but to changes in the organization of schooling, such as reducing class size. The failure of the positive results of the Tennessee STAR experiment to be reproduced in California points to the critical role that sustained attention to context and causal mechanisms can play. It also points to the value and importance of detailed study of what actually is going on in the classroom.

In some cases, contextual factors contributing to success or failure may be complex. But they can also be quite straightforward, as a study of the implementation of the Everyday Math curriculum adopted by the Pittsburgh schools suggests (Briars and Resnick, 2000). The study documented that Everyday Math improved student outcomes impressively, but only in some schools. More detailed analysis of results showed that the largest performance gains occurred in what the authors call "strong implementation" schools, where principals and teachers embraced the new pedagogical approach. In many schools, organizational commitment and support appear not to have been present and central office staff were often unwilling to confront those who were not fully implementing the new—and not yet locally proven—program. In these schools, performance effects were negligible (see Box 1.3). These findings suggest the importance of designing research to illuminate why innovations work.

Finally, replication of research findings is a canon of good science. But without a research infrastructure to ensure that it is a priority, it can be easily overlooked. For researchers establish-

BOX 1.3 Everyday Mathematics

In 1992, the Pittsburgh Public School District adopted a plan to align standards, tests, curricula, instructional materials, and professional development. Beginning in 1993, a new elementary school mathematics curriculum, Everyday Mathematics, was introduced (University of Chicago School Mathematics Project, 1995). This is a closely scripted curriculum for grades K-5 that is informed by research on early cognitive development. The program is directly mapped to the National Council of Teachers of Mathematics standards (1989) and closely aligned to the Pittsburgh Core Curriculum Framework for math (National Council of Teachers of Mathematics, 1989, 2000). Implementation began with the children entering kindergarten in 1993-1994; by 1997-1998, they were fourth graders.

In the 1996-1997 school year, the Pittsburgh Reform in Mathematics Education project (PRIME) began to offer extensive professional development for teachers and administrators. PRIME was designed explicitly to develop teachers' capacity to implement Everyday Mathematics; it provides in-class support including demonstration lessons, joint planning, and coaching, as well as after-school and summer workshops. Standards-based tests that reflected the three core curricular goals (skills, concepts, and problem solving) were given to fourth graders beginning in 1996. Briars and Resnick examined fourth grade mathematics achievement scores citywide over the three years from 1996 to 1998.* The 1998 fourth graders were the first cohort to have experienced the Everyday Math program throughout their elementary schooling.

By 1998, performance improved dramatically. Between 1996 and 1998, the percentage of students who met the district achievement standard in the Skills category increased from 30 to 52 percent. Seen from another vantage point, the good news is that the percentage of students at the very lowest of the five achievement categories on the skills subtest fell from 23 percent in 1966 to only 7 percent in 1998. There were substantial, if more modest, gains in the percentage of students meeting the standard in concepts and problem solving as well, although starting from a much lower 1996 baseline (8 percent).**

But there is a larger point to this story. If one looks at the data school by school rather than citywide, the degree of administrative and teacher support for the new system emerges as critical to the performance gains evident from 1996 to 1998. As Figure 1.2 illustrates, the schools with strong implementation showed dramatic improvement in all three areas, while in the schools with weak implementation there was little change from year to year on any of the measured achievement dimensions.

*The norm-referenced tests previously used in the district were also administered. We focus here on the New Standards assessment results.
**This reflects the concentration of the traditional math curriculum in the U.S. on computational skills; teachers and students alike needed to learn much more about mathematical concepts and problem solving.

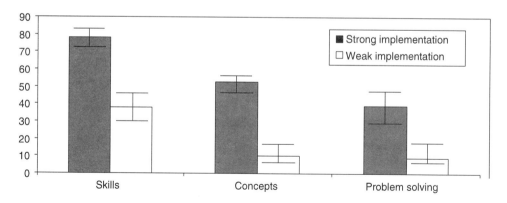

FIGURE 1.2 SOURCE: Briars and Resnick (2000:27).

ing a reputation, it has little cachet. For funders looking for promising new ideas, it can seem an unexciting addition to a portfolio. Yet it is critical to knowledge accumulation. A stable program of research focused on consolidating knowledge can make this a priority in a way that is unlikely to happen otherwise. Replication, of course, can provide new insight when it is conducted in natural settings—as much of the envisioned work would be. Innovations that work in some settings, with some students, might well turn out to be ineffective with other students or teachers. Rather than taking inconsistent outcomes as evidence that the innovation should be abandoned as a failure, such findings should themselves be the target of analysis. Because there is no one best curriculum for all students, or all teachers, analyzing the conditions under which various innovations do and do not improve outcomes should be a part of the process of evaluation and of preparing teachers to employ new teaching practices.

Addressing the Complexity of the System

Excellent curricula and instructional materials are important, but educational practice is not embodied solely in the tools and protocols of the trade. Rather, instructional tools, teacher knowledge, and the organization of the school are interdependent. They serve as three legs of the stool supporting student learning. While each is analytically independent of the other two, the effectiveness of any one in supporting student achievement depends on the strength of the other two. This lesson has been demonstrated repeatedly in education reform efforts. Therefore, focusing research attention on one leg of the stool without simultaneously attending to the other two is a strategy that holds little promise for success.

A compelling example is provided by the implementation in the Pittsburgh schools of an algebra curriculum developed by researchers at Carnegie Mellon University. The positive results in experimental trials led the researchers to expect a far more significant impact of their curriculum than the test results showed. Upon investigation, the researchers discovered that the number of hours devoted to mathematics teaching for the students using the program was far below the time requirements for mastery. Without reorganizing the daily schedule of the students in the program, the gains that the curriculum could produce were marginal (Anderson, 1983). This example sharply illustrates the importance of understanding what is required to make a program work, the difficulties in identifying "replications," and the need for detailed observation of actual practice in order to come to understand what can make a program successful.

Making Knowledge Usable

There has been relatively little systematic accumulation, synthesis, and sense-making in the education research enterprise that practitioners and policy makers can turn to for help with decision making. Instead, there is a huge volume of unconnected and undigested material available, and no authoritative source of carefully screened and vetted research knowledge. As a consequence, even the most promising research-based curricula, the most effective programs, and the most important insights into human learning are often little known and have little effect on U.S. schools.

The U.S. Department of Education has recently funded the What Works Clearinghouse to provide an authoritative evaluation of educational interventions. If support for the activity and initial efforts to establish high-quality standards are sustained, it will make a valuable contribution to decision making. A SERP infrastructure can substantially enhance the quality of an effort like that of the What Works Clearinghouse in several respects. First, answers regarding what works depend critically on an understanding of the outcomes to be achieved. In reading comprehension, for example, standardized measures test recall of text detail. There is research to suggest, however, that recall is not the same as comprehending the meaning of text for purposes of problem solving, and it does not guarantee that the information recalled will actually be integrated with the students' existing knowledge. In fact, students who do best at recall may not be the same students who do best at deeper comprehension (Mannes and Kintsch, 1987; National Research Council, 2003b). The answer to the question regarding what works will therefore depend critically on the outcome measures used. An R&D infrastructure like SERP can pursue research on the nature of reading comprehension and its assessment that will support better answers to questions of what works (National Research Council, 2003b).

Second, the optimal usability of findings requires more than ready access to the knowledge base. Educators often hold conceptions of teaching and learning that are at odds with the scientific principles underlying well-developed instructional innovations (Palincsar et al., 1989). Teachers need opportunities to learn about the underlying conceptions in order to use the innovation well, and the more innovative the practice, the more challenging will be the teacher learning involved. A program of research on teacher learning coupled with an effort to communicate with teachers effectively about what works is likely to enhance the prospect that programs with demonstrated success will be used successfully when they are taken to scale.

Finally, teachers and administrators need opportunities to understand innovative practices in a way that permits them to estimate the fit with their schools and the institutional supports that are required for successful implementation. They need to know not only that a program works, but also for whom it works, under what conditions it works, and why it works. While the Clearinghouse will ask these questions, the research base to answer them is not currently available. A research program that can systematically pursue these questions for promising programs would substantially strengthen the effectiveness of the effort to provide schools with a knowledge base concerning successful programs and practices.

SERP CAPABILITIES

The challenges of effectively linking research and practice identified here help to define a set of capabilities that a SERP enterprise must have if it is to succeed in that endeavor. What would have to be in place for the Number Worlds curriculum, Reciprocal Teaching, or class-size reduction to be more fully developed and made widely useful across settings? What structure would make the resources residing in the disciplines of cognitive science, psychology, sociology, and economics more available to the improvement of educational practice? What would be necessary for the nation to cull knowledge from the naturally occurring variations in educational practice that could be broadly useful to policy makers? What kind of entity would enable the wisdom and knowledge of highly effective practitioners and administrators to be systematized, reviewed, verified, accumulated, and made public?

In order to maximize the value of promising education innovations, SERP would have to carry out a coordinated set of research and development activities designed to identify candidate pedagogical, curricular, systemic, or organizational innovations that are worthy of study. It then would need to examine these systematically with careful attention to the conditions under which they have their effects, the particular population of students who are likely to benefit from them, and the teacher learning and organizational supports that are required for their effective adoption and implementation.

In order to benefit from advances in the relevant disciplines, SERP would need to create incentives for researchers to work on problems that have a likelihood of informing educational practice. Furthermore, it would need to create incentives to keep researchers and practitioners involved through the often lengthy process of development, implementation, and adaptation so as to ensure continued learning from and about innovative practices. In addition, SERP would need to provide the arrangements under which mutually informative conversations between researchers and practitioners can occur, so as to ensure that researchers' questions are genuinely informed by the most burning issues of practice.

In order to capitalize on and learn from naturally occurring variations in practice, SERP would need a process for surfacing and vetting both problems and practices that are worthy of sustained study—for example, what teachers need to know to teach algebra II to all of their students, or to ensure subject-matter learning for secondary students with limited literacy skills; or the strategies that would inspire engagement in a rigorous curriculum. One approach might be to describe current approaches to solving these problems, in particular those used by highly effective practitioners, and then to organize systematic field trials of alternate approaches that seem promising. Naturally occurring variation in practices, for example, charter schools, new approaches to school finance, teacher learning communities, and comprehension strategy instruction, could similarly provide a source of organized learning if subjected to systematic comparison and analysis.

An organization with these capabilities would be a resource for those responsible for today's classrooms, as well as for those in charge of long-term reform efforts. It would by its design blur the traditional distinction between basic and applied research, helping practitioners to think more like researchers and researchers to appreciate the challenges of practice. To accomplish its mission, it would need a process for selecting among the many possible research activities, for prioritizing commitments, and for consulting with a full array of stakeholders. It would need to create research environments in which student learning, teaching, and school organization can be studied simultaneously. And it must develop a capacity to reach those communities that can make use of the fruits of its efforts.

How SERP Relates to Other Efforts

As the first report of the SERP initiative made clear (see National Research Council, 1999:17-20), the Strategic Education Research Partnership we propose, although different from other research and reform efforts, is emphatically not a replacement for them. For the SERP idea to come to life, education leaders will have to see its potential for leveraging existing investments by the federal government, state governments, school systems, and private-sector organizations. The U.S. Department of Education, the National Science Foundation, and the National Institute of Child Health and Human Development have important ongoing programs supporting research and education reform. Likewise, major private foundations have long been working to improve education. In our view, a sustained and focused strategic research and development program like SERP can strengthen and leverage these efforts, helping them to realize their goals and bringing greater coherence and staying power to the whole.

In the sectors in which research has had a substantial impact on practice (and vice versa), it is well understood that research and development is an ongoing process, an unfolding of knowledge and understanding, marked now and then by important breakthroughs, producing new products along the way, revising and backtracking as effects are better understood. Close interaction between research and practice is important both to enable proposals developed in research to be tested and adjusted so that they can work in practice, and to enable researchers to understand the problems, puzzles, and constraints of the operational environment. The research investment takes years, even decades, to reach fruition. The history of investment in education research, with some notable exceptions, is one marked by impatience and abandonment of research endeavors in a relatively short time frame.

The pressure for immediate results is not surprising when education research takes place largely within the confines of a political institution. Voters whose children are in the public schools want those schools to improve their performance now. A 10- or 15-year time horizon is, from a parent's point of view, entirely useless. Because education is perceived as so central to the future opportunities of today's children, a focus on what can produce results in the short run is demanded of those in a new administration. And it is entirely understandable for each new administration to put its mark on education improvement by emphasizing what it will do differently—what it sees as potential paths to improvement.

What is needed is a program of research that proceeds from an understanding of how students learn, to research on the design and testing of instructional tools and programs, to replication in a range of contexts, to a study of teacher knowledge requirements, and finally, to an examination of the organizational requirements that support instruction and teacher learning. Without such sustained attention, research-based knowledge cannot accumulate and grow more sophisticated, and the potential contribution of research to practice cannot be realized.

A successful SERP research enterprise working at some remove from the political arena could serve as a significant asset to the existing education and education research agencies. Like the core holdings in an investment portfolio, SERP would represent long-term positions, accumulating steadily over time, which the nation holds for years. SERP would anchor the "managed portfolios" of political leaders or private philanthropies. Whatever the goals for educational improvement of a particular political administration, the availability of a solid research foundation would facilitate policy making. Whatever the particular education reform interests of foundations—be it urban schools or small schools or improving the prospects of minority and disadvantaged youth—the accumulating SERP data on learning, instruction, and schools as organizations would help them shape their action programs; partnering with SERP would help improve their investments.

If SERP had existed when Congress mandated the Statewide Systemic Initiative in 1990, for example, the National Science Foundation could have turned to SERP for an integrated knowledge base on the barriers to change in complex organizations, or effective organizational and environmental supports for academic learning.

If a future administration were to decide to pursue a reform agenda like Reading First, with its legislative mandate that state grant recipients implement research-based reading programs, SERP could provide the states with critically needed information about the characteristics of high-quality curricula and with examples of curricula that had been tested in various school settings. SERP could also produce research-based information on the teacher knowledge and teacher training associated with the effective use of a given curriculum.

To take another example, the Gates Foundation is presently devoting major resources to a small-school experiment in the state of Washington. To understand under what conditions size makes a difference or how to take optimal advantage of small school size, it might engage SERP in a systematic exploration of the contributions of size, curriculum, teacher quality/professional development, and other factors critical to student performance. Over the long term, this should significantly increase the payoff of its experiment in education.

If a strong SERP existed, some of the heat could be removed from the education debates that presently tend to cripple progress in education. A SERP enterprise one step removed from politics could take on questions about theories of learning or the efficacy of different instructional approaches (basic skills versus inquiry-based, phonics versus whole language) and subject such questions to systematic study. These questions are answerable. While policy positions will not—and should not—be determined by research outcomes alone, they should be informed by scientific research on learning, and by data on the relative effectiveness of various programs for various kinds of children and the conditions that maximize effectiveness.

In sum, SERP will offer action-oriented program links to the best research knowledge. It will offer funding agencies and foundations productive ways to work at the intersection of research and practice. It will offer those who worry about training future leaders of the research and education establishments an opportunity to create new careers that grow out of the interaction of research and practice, while providing for productive collaboration with the other parts of the education research enterprise. But most importantly, it will offer teachers, administrators, and state policy makers a steadily improving knowledge base to support them in their critical mission of educating the nation's children.

In the chapters that follow, we offer the committee's proposal for the design of an organization with the capabilities to carry out the broad SERP mission, a vision of how such an organization would attract the participation and funding needed for success, and illustrative examples of the kind of work the enterprise might undertake. But before we turn to that discussion, we address an even more fundamental question: would an infrastructure like the proposed SERP make a significant difference in teaching and learning? Although proof cannot be provided a priori, we devote Chapter 2 to examples that make a powerful case that such an infrastructure would considerably enhance the productivity of the education system.

2| Helping Hercules: Why Infrastructure Matters

Would the substantial investment required to build a new education research and development infrastructure pay off? Proof, of course, cannot be provided by arguments made in advance of such an experiment. But our case for such an investment rests on evidence that: (a) the collaborative research and development effort in school settings that we propose is feasible; (b) there are cases in which this type of research and development has been carried out with productive results that are directly applicable to improving classroom practice; and (c) this type of work, even when highly successful, has been difficult to sustain without the proposed research and development infrastructure.

To support these claims, we provide a set of illustrative cases below. The cases differ substantially in their details, but all were pioneering efforts; the individuals involved had to find paths through unfamiliar, and at times difficult, terrain. The researchers involved had to become a jack-of-all-trades, able to function in the separate worlds of research and practice, to design and conduct research, develop and maintain partnerships, and continue to raise substantial funds. And the efforts continue only so long as the individuals who undertook them do not tire and their funders do not shift focus. There are no railroads or highways that have been built in these pioneer's footsteps. Without a supporting infrastructure, their paths did not become well-traveled roads, and the settlements they created are unlikely to become permanent.

BOSTON READING STUDY

In 1996 the Boston public school system, with substantial foundation support, introduced a whole school reform program focused on primary grade literacy. Participating schools were required to adopt a structured model for literacy instruction from a menu of four options: Balanced Early Literacy (BEL), Developing Literacy First (DLF), Literacy Collaborative (LC), and Success for All (SFA). In the 1998-1999 school year, 66 schools were involved in the effort. The variation in the programs adopted, as well as the number of schools involved, provided an opportunity to learn a great deal about which programs produce which results, whether the program results differ for children with different demographic and primary language characteristics, and how teachers and administrators use the programs and their professional development components.

A research study was designed to examine these questions in Boston. In 1998, with initial funding from Harvard University's Interfaculty Initiative, Lowry Hemphill and Terrence Tivnan began pilot work in two schools that later expanded to a study of 16 schools—4 schools using each of the 4 models. The study was designed to examine how students perform on the separate skills that are known to contribute to success in early reading: word reading, word attack, phonemic awareness, writing, and reading comprehension (Tivnan, 2002).

While individual program effects are being studied in this ongoing program of research, so are the differences in instructional practices between and within programs. Data on student performance are collected, along with data on student characteristics and characteristics of the instructional program. Importantly, data will be collected over multiple years. Since reading is a skill that is still emerging in first grade, results of the program at the end of second and third grade will be critical to an informative program assessment.

Early findings already suggest that many important lessons are being learned about the programs and their role in teaching and learning, as well as about research on classroom practice. With regard to the programs themselves, their implementation has made a measurable difference. The biggest gains were in decoding and in reading sight words. No program could be deemed best overall. As one might expect, the programs that spent more time on developing phonemic awareness skills showed better results in tests of this skill, while programs that spent more time on language development showed relative strength in vocabulary and reading comprehension. More importantly, however, the differences in outcome for the same program in different classrooms were larger than the differences between programs. This is not an effect that can be attributed to the school, since large differences exist within a school as well. The research team is observing teachers' instructional practices in order to develop and test hypotheses about the contributors to differences in teacher effectiveness.

The preliminary results point to another important issue: the programs as a group post substantial gains in bringing students up to grade level in word reading, but they make far less progress in narrowing the yawning gap in reading comprehension and vocabulary. While the programs differ somewhat in their emphasis on these skills, none provides an adequate response to the existing disparities. For public policy and for the direction of future research and development dollars, this is a very important finding.

WOULD SERP MAKE A DIFFERENCE?

The research now under way in these Boston schools is an example of the type of research that can help inform education practice and policy. Indeed, the research team is working with teachers in the schools to provide professional development based on what is being learned about effective instructional practices. The schools involved in the project are eager for input from the researchers both for understanding the program outcomes and for informing instructional practice.

But while this case provides optimism regarding the potential of collaborations between researchers and practitioners, it also points to the inefficiencies and disincentives of carrying out this work in the absence of a supportive infrastructure. Without a formal organizational arrangement between the research team and Boston public schools, the researchers themselves must negotiate arrangements with each of the 16 schools. Those arrangements depend on personal relationships, and with each personnel change, the relationship must be renegotiated. The researchers also needed to obtain the parental permissions required to collect information on individual students for this type of research.

At the same time, the researchers have needed to secure the funds required to carry the project forward. The funding has come in one- or two-year commitments, requiring persistent attention to negotiating the next research grant or contract. In the early stages of the project, the researchers were also required to negotiate with the developers of each of the four programs regarding the outcome measures that would be used to assess program impact.

If SERP were in existence, funding, research protocols and instruments, and the terms of access to schools would still need to be negotiated, and permission to collect data on individual students would still need to be obtained. But an organization could develop the capacity to do these much more efficiently by institutionalizing the knowledge and skills involved and making routine what otherwise must be reinvented by each research team. Many outstanding researchers would be unable or unwilling to undertake the Herculean efforts of the Boston research team, discouraging this type of badly needed investigation.

The role of a SERP enterprise is not just facilitative. It would develop and steer a program that could make more of research findings. The Boston researchers are keenly aware of the opportunities lost by working in isolation. While many other jurisdictions around the country are using the same literacy programs in different contexts, the lack of a coordinated effort means that they are learning less about the features of those contexts that contribute to outcomes. The confidence in particular outcomes would be strengthened or called into question if results from other sites could be compared. But such a comparison requires an extent of coordination in research design that does not now exist.

Hemphill and Tivnan write up their results and present them at research conferences. They point out, however, that the operative norms at these meetings are not those of a network of researchers engaged in an effort to collectively advance a field, but rather those of a professional competition that minimizes the opportunity for productive collaboration. In their view, the role of a SERP network in fostering an environment in which the operative norms are those of productive collaboration would make a significant contribution to the productivity of work like theirs. The benefits of that collaboration, of course, would extend beyond researchers. A critical role for SERP would be one of supporting collaboration and shared knowledge among the school systems and teachers undertaking reforms to address similar problems (based in part on phone conversation with Lowry Hemphill, November 2002).

RECIPROCAL TEACHING

As the Boston reading study results confirm, many students who successfully learn to read nonetheless do poorly at reading comprehension. Instructional approaches to improving reading comprehension primarily fall under the category of strategy instruction (RAND, 2002a). The skills taught in strategy instruction generally target improved recall of text, teaching students to attend to headings, to outline or map the text in graphic form, and to reread for specific information or structural cues. While these strategies do improve recall, particularly for low-achieving students (National Institute of Child Health and Human Development, 2000), they focus on surface features of the text. They can therefore be mastered successfully without the student understanding the meaning of the text or integrating the new knowledge from the text with their existing understandings.

Reciprocal Teaching (RT) is a technique developed by Annemarie Palincsar and Anne Brown two decades ago to engage students more deeply in understanding the meaning of text. The active processes of making sense of a text involved in skilled reading comprehension are taught to students explicitly.[1] The teacher initially models four strategies: questioning unclear content, summarizing meaning paragraph by paragraph, clarifying comprehension problems, and predicting what will come next. Students practice the strategies with guidance from the teacher, and, as their skill increases, the teacher increases the demands. Gradually the role of the teacher diminishes as students become more competent and sophisticated in the questioning and monitoring role. In groups, students ask each other

---

[1]For more detail, see the companion report, *Learning and Instruction: A SERP Research Agenda.*

questions, practicing aloud the type of dialogue that will eventually become internal.

The technique has been used to improve listening comprehension among young children, as well as to improve reading comprehension once children become fluent readers. Children who are exposed to the reciprocal teaching intervention performed better than control children on several dimensions, including the quality of summaries and questions and scores on criterion tests of comprehension (Palincsar and Brown, 1984). Gains were maintained over time, generalized to classroom comprehension tests, and transferred to novel tasks involving summarizing, questioning, and clarifying.

WOULD SERP MAKE A DIFFERENCE?

Reciprocal Teaching has demonstrable effects on a problem that is at the heart of effective education. The ability to comprehend text unlocks knowledge in all fields. But without an infrastructure to nurture the program through further stages of development and integration into the classroom, Reciprocal Teaching has largely remained a small-scale effort in the hands of a dedicated researcher whose work has moved into new areas. The absence of any infrastructure to carry the program forward has repercussions that Annemarie Palincsar describes vividly:

> Believe it or not, after all these many years, I still get requests (at least two a month) to conduct professional development regarding reciprocal teaching. I always feel badly saying no (in part because a very important reason for doing the research was to inform practice), and I really have no one to whom I can refer the school personnel with confidence that the version of RT that they will describe/demonstrate is consistent with the original RT. . . . Because there is currently nothing like SERP, I had no systematic way to disseminate RT on a large scale nor to engage in professional development that would reach the numbers of schools and districts that have requested it.

> This is what I did do. . . . I authored a facilitator's manual (that has been sent to literally thousands of folks who have requested it). . . . I also prepared a videotape that provides an overview of RT, excerpts of a teacher implementing RT, and debriefing conversations with students who have learned how to use RT. I purchased a tape-to-tape video recorder and when people ask for this video tape, I ask them to send me a blank VHS tape in a stamped, self-

addressed padded envelope and I make them a copy of this tape. I have lost count of how many copies I have made but I should be embarrassed to send any more since it is so dated!

What role might a SERP have played? Well, first, it would have been wonderful to have had high-quality video and audio of teachers working in different contexts (demographically as well as content-wise) using RT in a manner that reflects the principles on which it was designed.

Second, it would have been so satisfying to never have had to say "no" to a professional development request because there was a network of teacher leaders or professional development personnel who would either work onsite or who would have offered teaching institutes to support educators and educational leaders to learn about RT (and other forms of comprehension instruction).

Third, it would have been ideal to be able to have supported conversations with other researchers who were similarly investigating class-wide models of comprehension instruction to talk about how our work was complementary and where it differed and the implications of these differences for professional development. For example, what support can we provide educators who are trying to choose among QtA [Questioning the Author] (Beck et al., 1997), Collaborative Reasoning with Text (Chinn and Anderson and colleagues), SAIL (Pressley et al., 1989) and RT? How might we have done our research more synergistically so that we might have learned more from our respective programs of research? I can imagine an entity like SERP playing such a role.

Palincsar describes an effort by a major commercial publishing company to conduct professional development on RT, with neither her permission (which is not required), nor her input. Her understanding is that the version of RT taught in the training program is fundamentally different from hers in critical dimensions. But no one at the company has returned her phone calls. She writes:

Fourth. . . it would have been terrific to have some means of working more closely with commercial endeavors, so that these efforts do not undermine the research and development the publisher is trying to disseminate.

A major national goal expressed in the No Child Left Behind legislation is effective reading instruction for all children. Millions of dollars are earmarked to support the effort. But without a research and development infrastructure, one of the few interventions that has been demonstrated to improve reading comprehension outcomes will reach children only if a teacher learns about the program, contacts Annemarie Palincsar—and mails a self-addressed, stamped enveloped with a blank tape inside (Annemarie Palincsar, Charles Walgreen Professor of Reading and Literacy, School of Education, University of Michigan, personal communication, November 2002).

CREATING THE COGNITIVE TUTOR

The Cognitive Tutor Algebra I is one of a set of "cognitive tutors" developed at Carnegie Mellon University to teach algebra and geometry. Of great relevance to the SERP vision, the tutors are a good illustration of how to make the transition from the laboratory to the classroom, as well as the nature of the partnership between researchers and teachers that have made the program a success.

The work at Carnegie Mellon began as a project to see whether a computational theory of thought, called ACT (Anderson, 1983), could be used as a basis for delivering computer-based instruction in algebra. The ACT theory of problem-solving cognition is the basis for modeling students' algebra knowledge. These models are capable of generating almost any sensible solution to an algebra problem. They are embedded in a computer program that can then identify the particular approach a student is taking to a solution.

The cognitive models enable two sorts of instructional responses that are individualized to students:

1. By a process called model tracing, the program will infer how a student is going about problem solving and generate appropriate help and instruction when a student is pursuing an unproductive or incorrect strategy.
2. By a process called knowledge tracing, the program will infer where a student falls in the learning trajectory (what knowledge has been mastered and what is insecure) and select instruction and problems appropriately.

Developing cognitive models that accurately reflect student competences and developing appropriate instructional responses is very much an iterative process. The success of the tutors depends on a design-test-redesign effort in which models are assessed for how well they capture competence and in which instructional responses are assessed for effectiveness.

In controlled trials, the curriculum performs well. It was found that students could go through the algebra curriculum with the Tutor in a third of the time normally required. In carefully managed classrooms, students would show about a standard deviation (approximately one letter grade) improvement in achievement (Anderson et al., 1995). In real classroom situations, the impact of the tutors tends not to be as large, varying from 0 to 1 standard deviation across 13 evaluations. Another third-party evaluation focused on the social consequences of the tutors; it documented large motivational gains resulting from the active engagement of students and their successful experiences on challenging problems (Schofield et al., 1990).

Unlike many such small-scale success stories in cognitive science, this project was able to grow to the point at which the cognitive tutors now are used in 33 of the 100 largest school districts in the United States and are interacting with about 200,000 students yearly. A number of features were critical to making this successful transition:

1. While the ACT theory provided the foundation for the program, there was a concerted effort to identify a curriculum that educators wanted taught in the classroom. In particular, there was a major effort to teach a curriculum that was in compliance with the National Council of Teachers of Mathematics standards (National Council of Teachers of Mathematics, 1989).

2. A curriculum was designed that teachers would accept and could implement. The curriculum design was largely the product of teachers with experience in urban classrooms. To meet their needs, a full-year curriculum was developed rather than an enrichment program to be inserted into an existing curriculum. And the computer tutors were used as a support rather than a replacement for the teachers. In this curriculum

students spend 40 percent of their time with the computer tutors and 60 percent of their time with other activities. These classroom activities help them transition to their lessons with the tutor, as well as to transition from the tutor to things that they will have to do in the real world.

3. A structure was set up for supporting the use of the curriculum and tutors. Before introducing the tutors into a classroom, it has been important to provide professional development time to enable teachers to prepare for the change they are about to experience. A center at Carnegie Mellon was set up for responding to teacher and school problems. As the adoptions grew, a separate company (Carnegie Learning Corporation) was created to perform this function and maintain and adapt the materials.

4. Ultimately, such a curriculum must be financially self-sustaining, and the program was developed from the beginning with a plausible financial model in mind. In particular, by offering a full grade 9-11 curriculum, it was possible to earn the kind of income from sales that is necessary to sustain the activity.

WOULD SERP MAKE A DIFFERENCE?

The Cognitive Tutor Algebra I represents a success of the type that is rare in K-12 education. Its developers, however, point to the problems raised when an effort like this is undertaken without a research infrastructure:

Once leaving the laboratory, there have been only haphazard efforts to evaluate the curriculum as it has multiplied through the school systems. It is only now that our tutors are about to receive their first adequate third-party evaluation and this is only because of the funding from the Hewlett Foundation. There are natural reasons to avoid rigorous evaluation of material. Early in the development of a program a negative evaluation may make it difficult to get the next round of funding. Once a product becomes commercial as ours did, there is even less incentive for such evaluations because in addition to bringing potentially bad news, they cost and so threaten the need to meet the next month's payroll. Mechanisms need to be set up to both require and fund rigorous formative evaluations in the development of curricula, and impartial third-party evaluations of curricula once they start to be disseminated.

And despite its success, Anderson argues that the Cognitive Tutor Algebra I has room for improvement in some very important dimensions.

> Early in the development of the algebra tutor, a decision was made to place a heavy emphasis on contextualizing algebra to help students make the transition to the formalism. This has been successful and there are fewer students dropping out. However, as a consequence the curriculum does not achieve the fluency in symbol manipulation and abstract analysis expected for high-achieving students. There is no reason why the cognitive tutors could not be extended to these topics but they have not (from *Learning and Instruction: A SERP Research Agenda*, Box 3.3).

THE COGNITIVE TUTOR ALGEBRA I IN AN OKLAHOMA SCHOOL DISTRICT

Pat Morgan, mathematics coordinator for the Moore Independent School District in Oklahoma, knew Carnegie Learning Corporation's Cognitive Tutor Algebra I had been rated favorably by the U.S. Department of Education. She thought it was worth a try in her school district but knew from experience that her teachers were likely to balk at being asked to do something new. She decided that, to get their support, she would need to show them that the new program worked better than their current program. Her plan was to introduce the Cognitive Tutor Algebra I in a subset of the algebra classrooms, and compare the results to those in the classrooms that continued to use McDougal Littell's Heath algebra I text.

With a Goals 2000 grant from the U.S. Department of Education, Pat was able to purchase the program and pay teachers to attend training workshops during the summer of 2000. In September, the Cognitive Tutor Algebra I was introduced in five middle schools in the district. Students in the honors algebra class were not involved in the study. Other students had already been assigned more or less randomly to classes, and teachers who had undergone training were asked to teach both traditional classes and Cognitive Tutor Algebra I classes so that the effect of the teacher could be separable from the effect of the program. In order to compare outcomes, Pat decided to use a standardized, end-of-course assessment developed by the Educational Testing Service (ETS).[2]

At the end of the school year, scores were obtained for 220 students who received traditional algebra instruction and 224 who received instruction with the Cognitive Tutor Algebra I. The data were turned over to the Carnegie Learning Corporation for analysis. Students who received traditional instruction earned a mean scaled score of 15.1 (with a standard deviation of 5.5); students instructed with Cognitive Tutor earned 16.7 (with a stand deviation of 5.7). This indicates a benefit from the Cognitive Tutor Algebra I that is significant ($F(1,442) = 8.8$, $p < 0.01$). When student performance was broken down by category—minimal, basic, proficient, and advanced—the nature of the gains is more apparent. The Cognitive Tutor Algebra I reduced substantially the number of students who performed at the lowest levels and almost doubled the percentage who were proficient. It had no effect, however, on those who scored at the advanced level. Grade point averages were higher for students who used the tutor, as were scores on a student attitude survey. With the exception of the honors algebra classes, teachers in all algebra classes in the school district now use the Carnegie Learning curriculum willingly.

WOULD SERP HAVE MADE A DIFFERENCE?

The introduction of the Cognitive Tutor Algebra I in the Moore school district suggests that a well-designed test of whether a curriculum improves student outcomes can stimulate productive change. It also suggests that the conditions for such a study, including random assignment and intrateacher program comparisons, can be created in normal school settings.

But for school district personnel to manage such an effort without the support of a research infrastructure requires an extraordinary effort. While Pat Morgan undertook that effort, it was not one she could sustain. The answers provided by the study were helpful, but Pat and her math teachers would like to know whether the gains for the Cognitive Tutor Algebra I students are sustained in higher-level math courses. And she observes that teachers using the curriculum are beginning to adapt

---

[2]The test scores are reported on a 0-50 scale, and the national mean scores for the select group of students who take this test is 18.

it somewhat. She would like to understand the consequences of the adaptations. But with tight budgets, she cannot afford to have ETS administer the end-of-year test anymore. The school district is now also experimenting with Carnegie Learning's Cognitive Tutor Algebra II and with the Cognitive Tutor Geometry on a small scale, but they are not conducting a similar study. While Pat would like to continue to study program effects to better inform her decisions, her job as the math coordinator is very demanding, and she cannot undertake the effort to raise funds and conduct additional studies on her own again. Even more than the money, she says, she needs help so that the unfamiliar job of researcher does not fall fully on her shoulders.

Pat Morgan's research design was better than she knew. She had no background in research. She just believed from experience that the teacher is the most important contributor to student achievement, so she decided that she needed to have the same teachers using both curricula. Students who were not assigned to honors algebra had been placed without tracking into other sections of algebra before a decision was made regarding which teachers would introduce the new curriculum in which of their classes, so random assignment was happenstance. Once the data were collected, Pat wasn't sure how to make the best use of them, so she called Carnegie Learning and found help on that score. She provided one of the best tests of the curriculum to date, as well as a valuable source of information for other school districts considering the program, although that outcome was not by design.

A research and development infrastructure prepared to support efforts like this and to guide research design could make more commonplace what is now the outcome of the combination of happenstance and extraordinary effort by a very dedicated and insightful school administrator. It could also make the very instructive finding from one school district easily available to other districts, so that thousands of other Pat Morgans could persuade their teachers of the value of trying a new instructional approach (Pat Morgan, mathematics coordinator, Moore Independent School District, Moore, Oklahoma, personal communication, November 2002).

LINKING RESEARCH AND PRACTICE WITH EASE

One Wednesday morning in 1998, Catherine Snow arrived in her office to find a large box. It contained many sheaves of test data, summarized in a few tables, and a note that read something like this:

> I collected these data in the Title I program of the White Bear Lake Schools—we designed an intervention program based on your findings from the Home-School Study of Language and Literacy Development. The results seem to suggest it worked. But I don't know how to do the right analyses, so I am sending you the data.

Snow got in touch with the source of the note and the data, Gail Jordan, who was then Title I director in White Bear Lake. Gail is a gifted curriculum designer and teacher educator, with a commitment to using research results to inform practice. Gail had taken seriously the correlational findings reported by Snow and her colleagues suggesting that preschool and kindergarten-age children in low-income families did better in literacy learning if they had had rich linguistic interactions with their parents. The helpful interactions that the researchers described included telling stories, reading books and engaging in discussion about them, giving explanations, using rich vocabulary, and engaging in pretend play. Relying heavily on the research findings, Gail figured out how to teach parents to engage in these sorts of interactions and how to design activities that kindergarten teachers could assign as homework that would provide occasions for the parent. She also met with the research team before designing the program.

With a Ph.D. under her belt, Gail also designed and carried out a random assignment study—randomly assigning kindergarten classrooms to treatment and control conditions, pretesting all the children in order to be able to control for initial status, and incorporating ways of assessing how many of the activities parents engaged in. She was engaging in precisely the kind of problem-oriented, practice-embedded research that is needed to improve education, and she successfully designed and carried out a very sophisticated study. She did not, however, know how to analyze the results or write up the findings for broader dissemination. Fortunately, she passed along the data, rather than just leaving them in the corner of her office.

Snow had some uncommitted funds for doctoral student support available, so she hired Michelle Porche to analyze the dataset. Michelle's analysis confirmed, as Gail's preliminary look at the findings had suggested, that the group that had received the intervention showed greater gains in language skills over the course of their kindergarten year and, furthermore, that those gains were greatest for the children who had started with the weakest language skills. Gail Jordan subsequently visited Snow and Porche, and they worked together on writing up the paper. It was published in *Reading Research Quarterly* as "Project EASE: Easing Children's Transition to Kindergarten Literacy Through Planned Parent Involvement." It won the International Reading Association award for the best paper published in that journal in the year 2000. Porche also helped Jordan build a web site describing EASE and providing resources for those who wanted to replicate it; EASE is now being used widely in low-income districts in the United States, and it has been incorporated into a state literacy reform initiative in Ohio (where it is again being evaluated).

WOULD SERP HAVE MADE A DIFFERENCE?

The outcome in the EASE case was a very positive one from all standpoints. The important work done both by a practitioner and by researchers came together in a way that allowed both practice, and the knowledge base, to advance. But while the success is worthy of celebration, it is disquieting that so many of the critical events were a matter of chance, as Snow makes clear:

> Many events had to converge to enable EASE to be disseminated and implemented outside White Bear Lake. First, Gail Jordan is more focused on the possibilities of research than many practitioners—though of course in an ideal world every educational innovation initiated locally would be subjected to a systematic evaluation. Second, Gail and I had met before, so she felt she could send me the data. Third, I happened to have some uncommitted funds that could support analysis of the data. Fourth, I happened to have a doctoral student interested in parent involvement and in literacy, who could thus easily be recruited to be involved in this project. Fifth, the findings were of sufficient interest that *Reading Research Quarterly* was willing to publish them. Sixth, the intervention was designed in such a way that it

was feasible for others to replicate it without much adaptation. If any one of these factors had been different, this valuable educational intervention with its potential to improve children's literacy success would never have seen the light of day.

Gail Jordan also notes how easily the value of this work could have been compromised.

> It was a challenge to keep the integrity of the project because the planning team had no research background and there were many times that there were confounding suggestions made (like making experimental classrooms full day and control classrooms half day). There were also concerns about the amount of testing required. . . . It would have been wonderful to have a research team guide us in those key decisions. . . . Our success was truly due to the kindness of strangers, specifically the research team at Harvard (Gail Jordan, personal communication, December 2002).

Surely there are many other cases in which locally designed innovations remain local and person-specific because some or all of the chance events were absent. The purpose of SERP is to make what is now an extraordinary outcome much more commonplace. It would do so by providing the infrastructure to connect practitioners like Gail Jordan to senior researchers like Catherine Snow and more junior researchers like Michelle Porche. It would provide support for the design of an intervention to assure replicability, as well as for the design of program evaluation to ensure rigor, relying less on extraordinary capacities of those in Gail Jordan's role.

In a world with a well-functioning SERP organization, progress would not require that the developer of the intervention have the capacity to design a random assignment trial on her own, as was true in this case. And SERP would have extensive capacity for data analysis so that high-quality data collection efforts, to be used, would not require the good fortune of a researcher with financial and human capital to spare. Finally, SERP would engage the effort to make the EASE results available more widely to those who are unlikely to read a report of published research (Catherine Snow, Henry Lee Shattuck Professor of Education, Harvard Graduate School of Education, personal communication, December 2002).

CONSORTIUM ON CHICAGO SCHOOL RESEARCH

Perhaps the most powerful evidence to suggest the possibility and the value of research on practice, conducted in school settings as collaborative efforts among researchers, practitioners, and policy makers, comes from the Consortium on Chicago School Research. The consortium began in 1990 under the leadership of Anthony Bryk as an effort to study the impact of a major school reform effort passed into law in Chicago in 1988. The mission of the consortium is to undertake research of high technical quality that can inform education policy making and school improvement efforts.

The 1988 Chicago school reform decentralized authority and accountability in the schools. It established local school councils (LSCs) for that purpose, comprised of the school's principal, two teachers, and six elected parents.[3] The LSCs approved the budget and held authority over the principal's contract. All schools were required to develop, implement, monitor, and update annually a school improvement plan (SIP), with LSC participation and oversight (Consortium on Chicago School Research, 2003).

The consortium's initial task was to study what happened in the wake of the reform. From the outset, this required comprehensive data collection. Since 1991 the consortium has conducted biannual surveys of students, teachers, and principals. Through an agreement with the Chicago Public Schools, its archives include the following:

- Test score data for the Iowa Tests of Basic Skills (ITBS), tests of academic proficiency, the Illinois Goal Assessment Program, and the Illinois Standards Achievement Test (beginning in the late 1980s);
- Administrative history information (as of 1992);
- Grade files from all high school students (as of 1993).

As part of a five-year grant from the Chicago Annenberg Research Project, the consortium also collected extensive data at

---

[3] In high schools, a student representative joined the group.

24 schools on teacher assignments, samples of student work, and extensive, in-depth interviews and classroom observations.

As the reforms in Chicago evolved, including a shift of authority from school boards to the mayor in 1994-1995 on a temporary basis, the consortium has continued to amass the data that will allow the effects to be teased out over time. The availability of this rich dataset has spawned many studies over the decade of importance for education policy. They have advanced understanding of schools as organizations and of the conditions that foster school improvement, providing critical insights on the effects of high school size, intraschool teacher relationships, and the cognitive demands placed on students by teachers.

The consortium has also worked with schools to provide them with data, and an approach to interpreting it, that give schools greater insight into their own functioning and performance. For example, the consortium's work allows each school with an eighth grade class to look at how its graduates perform over the course of the next five years. But the exchange between researchers and teachers is bidirectional. Important findings in studies of relational trust among school personnel have originated from the insights of teachers who felt that this played a major role in the performance of a school's students.

Many of the studies done by the consortium could serve to illustrate research that has provided critical knowledge and insights for policy makers, practitioners, or both. For example, the enactment of legislation in 1996 ending social promotion in the Chicago Public Schools set minimum scores in math and reading that students must achieve on the ITBS in grades 3, 6, and 8 in order to be promoted. Students who failed to meet the cutoff were required to attend a summer school program and retake the test at program completion. Students who fail again to meet the standard are retained in grade.

The Chicago policy was designed to address problems faced by all school districts. Many students are having difficulty in later grades, particularly high school, because they lack basic skills. Teachers are being asked to teach to higher standards. But many believe that the students who appeared in their classrooms do not have the skills to move on to more advanced work.

The "theory of action" in the legislation, according to the consortium research team, is three pronged (Roderick et al.,

1999). First, before students are tested, they, their parents, and their teachers face new incentives. When students are confronted with the prospect of being retained in grade, they are motivated to work harder, and their parents are motivated to monitor the student's performance more closely. Teachers are sent a strong message to focus attention on students who are not mastering basic skills and to emphasize those skills in their teaching. To improve the opportunity to succeed, students who are at risk of failure are given extended instructional time through Lighthouse, an after-school program begun in 1997.

The second prong provides an opportunity for a second chance. If a student fails to meet the minimum standard at the end of the school year, the summer bridge program offers additional, more focused instruction. The theory is that many students who fail initially can be brought up to speed with this additional opportunity. Finally, a second failure to meet the standard is met with retention in grade. The theory here is that students who repeat the material yet again will master it and move on to the next grade better prepared.

A research team at the consortium set out to test each of these theories. A full analysis will require data collection over a longer period of time to ascertain long-term effects, but results from the first few years are very informative (Roderick et al., 1998, 1999). Using 1995 data as a reference point, the policy raised the number of students meeting minimum standards in sixth and eighth grades (by 20 percent and 21 percent respectively, during the first year), and efforts both during the school year and the summer bridge program contributed. For third graders, there was no measured improvement during the school year, but some improvement after the Summer Bridge program. For all three grades results improved somewhat each year from 1997 to 1999. The students with the weakest skills at the start gained most. Between 1995 and 1997 the proportion of high-risk students who were able to meet the cutoff score rose from 4 to 34 percent among sixth graders and from 12 to 49 percent among eighth graders.

The picture is bleaker for students who were retained in grade. They did not do better than students who were previously socially promoted; only one-fourth of the eighth graders and one-third of the sixth and third graders stayed in the system and passed the test cutoff at the end of the repeated year. Results for third graders were particularly troublesome, since the program appeared to do harm to performance outcomes. Third graders below the cutoff had on average improved 1.5 grade equivalents (GEs) when socially promoted, but only 1.2 GEs when retained. For eighth graders, one-year dropout rates were higher with retention than with social promotion. Clearly, a policy that produces positive benefits for some students (those who meet the minimum standard) imposes very real costs on others (those who are retained).

The work of the consortium raised important policy questions, some of which have already sparked a response. Given the poor results for third graders, the additional support provided through the Lighthouse and Summer Bridge programs was extended to first and second graders whose performance was below grade level. And a search for more effective ways of addressing the needs of children who fail to meet the standard even after a summer program is now under way. The consortium report indicates: "CPS [Chicago Public Schools] has continued to experiment with alternatives to retention and with directing resources to students in the second [retained] year. At present, students in the retained year are provided with substantial extra resources through Lighthouse, reduced class sizes, and extra instructional support in schools hit hard by retention. In our subsequent work, we will be looking specifically at how these various interventions in the retained year. . . may shape students' learning" (Roderick et al., 1999:57).

The ability to follow students from one year to the next allowed for further insight. Third grade students who improved enough in the summer program to be promoted made gains in the next year at about the same inadequate pace as in the previous year, leaving them at risk of falling behind by the time of the next test. Students were not on a different learning trajectory; they simply were given a one-time boost from the summer program. The report authors write: "taken together, one interpretation of the findings of this report is that the CPS social promotion policy has worked to reveal a core problem—the adequacy of instruction during the school year. If this is indeed a problem, then the ultimate success of this policy will depend upon whether the extra program efforts and extra efforts on the part of students are matched with an increase in the capacity of teachers to build early literacy and numeracy and to diagnose and address students' problems when they are not progressing" (Roderick et al., 1999:57).

Future work planned at the consortium will include analysis of the instructional impact of the program—the extent to which the focus on raising ITBS scores in reading and math constrict instructional opportunities—as well as a cost analysis. Providing the Lighthouse and Summer Bridge programs has positive outcomes, but it is expensive. Would that money be more or less productive if it were invested in raising the quality of instruction during the regular school day? Given the emphasis nationwide on using high-stakes testing approaches to raising standards, the potential policy implications of this research in Chicago are vast.

WOULD SERP MAKE A DIFFERENCE?

The work of the consortium is of tremendous importance not only to Chicago, but also to all schools—particularly those in large, urban school districts. Despite the success of the consortium in conducting high-quality social science research that is directly applicable to education policy and practice, its long-term viability is in question. Its existence thus far has depended on three foundations that are based in Chicago. While all have been generous in their support, foundations do not typically fund long-term efforts. They expect that if an enterprise is successful, it will generate the capacity to be self-sustaining. And as the foundation leadership changes (as it has recently in all three of the supporting foundations), new ideas that bear the mark of the new president can overshadow ideas that emerged under previous leadership. At the same time that enthusiasm wanes for an enterprise that is no longer new, cost pressures begin to rise. Initially the work of the consortium drew on Ph.D. candidates who could be used at relatively low wages for purposes of helping to found something new and important. But to keep employees as they enter their long-term career paths, and as the institution becomes more established, will require more competitive salaries.

The consortium's leadership is uncertain about future funding. At the same time, however, they are encouraged by the expanding possibilities of the work they are undertaking. Their presence in the schools is more secure and welcomed. With permission from the school system, they will begin to collect new classroom-level data that will allow student performance to be studied in relation to individual programs and teachers.

This will create a much more powerful ability to study learning and instruction. A growing number of researchers have become interested in the uniquely rich data collected by the consortium and they are using it to productive ends. That so clearly valuable an effort finds itself in such a precarious position today speaks strongly to the inadequacy of the existing education research and development infrastructure.

Moreover, while the consortium's effort to work at the intersection of research, policy, and practice has been impressive, Bryk notes that they are "the only game in town." Chicago's approach to school reform is very different from approaches taken in many other districts and states. But we are not learning how the different approaches compare, because there are no comparison sites. "If there were a federation of consortia like ours," says Bryk, "the power of this work would be greatly magnified. We could really make some progress" (Anthony Bryk, Professor, University of Chicago, Department of Sociology, personal communication, December 2002).

A federation of field sites could lend power to education research and development in another respect as well: different field sites could begin with entirely different foci. The Chicago consortium began as an effort to draw on one of the three resources we highlighted in Chapter 1: natural experimentation. The experiment began with a policy change (decentralization). The study of the effects of that change quickly took researchers into issues of school organization (professional communities), teacher learning (professional development), and instruction (authentic intellectual work). The questions asked, however, were shaped by the framing question: What are the effects of the policy reform?

Other efforts that draw on different resources—that take as their point of departure the insights from disciplines related to student learning or teacher learning, for example—would probably look quite different. If the leading questions pertained to how students improve their reading comprehension or how they develop mathematical knowledge, the research agenda would have a stronger focus on the components of knowledge development and conceptual change. When those questions are pursued in the school context, teacher knowledge and learning, as well as the organization and policy influences on the classroom, are likely to play an important role in the research as well.

With different lead questions and different research expertise, the areas in which our understanding progresses are likely to be very different. While one agenda would be expected to yield insights about the locus of decision-making authority in the school district, the other is more likely to advance the knowledge base on effective reading comprehension instruction. The synergistic effects of the different efforts, brought together by the networking efforts of a SERP infrastructure, would lend a power to education research and development and its ability to inform policy and practice that is nowhere present today.

CONCLUSION

The above set of cases makes clear the possibility of conducting rigorous research on and for educational practice. But they also highlight the difficulty of undertaking and sustaining those efforts in the absence of a new research and development infrastructure. SERP would facilitate such efforts in the future by

- Providing a place for researchers and practitioners interested in research to link up;
- Providing institutional support for negotiating collaborations between researchers, school administrators, and teachers;
- Providing program steering and stable funding to allow successful efforts to be carried forward;
- Providing research and data collection protocols to limit the role of happenstance in the production of high-quality outcomes; and
- Providing regular opportunities for those involved in education research and development in different sites to learn from and build on each other's work.

3 The SERP Organization

What organizational structure for a SERP enterprise would allow it to successfully carry out the broad mission described in the opening chapter? The key design features we propose emerge from two overarching goals:

1. Developing and steering a research and development (R&D) program that is coherent, high quality, use-inspired, and cumulative and
2. Attracting stable funding and support.

After considering key design features that we believe would support those goals, we propose a SERP governance structure and a broad organizational design.

∙ ∙

DEVELOPING A PROGRAM

When the committee began its work, we had no common vision of a SERP organization. Rather quickly, however, agreement emerged on two central design features we judge to be critical to developing and executing the SERP program: (1) an organization with a strong center capable of steering the research and development program and assuring program utility and quality, and (2) dispersed field sites in which collaborative, use-inspired research can be carried out as part of a coherent program. The rationale for each is described below.

SERP Headquarters

Tapping existing resources to improve student learning, we argue, will require ongoing assessment of the opportunities presented by existing research, teaching practices, and innovations as well as making hard choices about where investment in further research and development is likely to have a high payoff. Once investments have been undertaken, carrying research and development through all of the stages necessary for utility in practice will require an ongoing assessment of program results and an active steering of the program over time in productive directions. This assessment and steering, if they are to lead to a coherent and cumulative program of research and development, will require a strong central SERP operation—an entity that we shall refer to as SERP headquarters.

Requirements for maintaining program quality further suggest the need for a strong center. We envision two mechanisms for supporting quality: one is oversight of research designs by a scientific advisory board to assess whether the questions asked can be adequately addressed by a proposed study. Much has been made in recent years about the methodological weakness of education research, and the debate about research methods has even been carried into the halls of Congress. This committee concurs with the National Research Council report on scientific standards in education research (National Research Council, 2002b) in believing that there is no one best methodology for education research. Rather, the method must be matched to the question. Oversight by a scientific advisory board would allow SERP to conduct and support research using a variety of methods, while at the same time addressing the problem of weak research design that has plagued the field.

The second venue for quality control we envision is oversight of the research products through rigorous peer review. While the peers who carry out the reviewing would be outside SERP in order to avoid a potential conflict of interest, the organization of peer review would need to be coordinated. Both the scientific advisory board and the coordination of the peer review would be the responsibility of SERP headquarters.

Finally, we have argued that to create a body of research that accumulates both across research projects and over time, uniform data collection efforts and common research protocols will be required. Moreover, since the mission of SERP is to improve student learning, the research program must concern itself from the outset with specifying and measuring educational outcomes and promoting the requisite integration of data across studies. Questions about what works, for whom, and under what circumstances are difficult to answer; the dimensions of context that are potentially important are many and are not simply measured. But prospects for progress on these critical issues are improved if the definition of "what works" includes outcomes carefully measured over time, if "for whom" includes a large array of relevant individual and group characteristics, and "under what circumstances" includes information on the schools, teachers, administrators, and resources that contribute to context.

Education research to date has been characterized by a marked absence of the sorts of shared standards, measurement protocols, and other techniques that are necessary for researchers to replicate and cross-validate findings. Without such research protocols and common measurement instruments, we cannot be sure whether positive results reflect attributes of a given intervention that can be generalized. Common measurement and research protocols are far more standard in other fields, like medicine, where advancing knowledge efficiently has been a priority for some time. Generating an atmosphere of productive collaboration among researchers through requirements placed on grant funding, as well as establishing and maintaining standards for data collection and for research and measurement protocols, are all critical activities for a SERP headquarters.

FIELD SITES

The defining features of the SERP research program are that it is collaborative and use-inspired, being research for, and often on, practice. It will therefore require the participation of teachers, administrators, and policy makers, as well as access to classrooms, schools, school districts, and possibly teacher education programs as "field sites." These are the equivalent of the teaching hospitals in medicine, places of practice that serve as sites for research. While we propose a strong SERP headquarters, the locations envisioned for most of the actual research and development would be widely dispersed.

Field sites occupy a central place in the SERP plan. They will provide a test bed for iterative research on learning, on teaching, on changes in school organization and culture to support learning, and on the development and use of tools and curriculum. In addition, they will be the ground for observation, articulation, and modeling of effective practice. They will demonstrate the effects of incorporating research-based programs, pedagogy, and organizational changes to practitioners and policy makers.

The field sites might well take many different forms, and, indeed, different types of sites would be suited to different research questions. An entire state may want to join the SERP partnership and itself become a field site for study of state-level policy change. One or more school districts, perhaps in collaboration with a local university, might constitute a site. Or a set of school districts dispersed across a state or across the nation might join together to work on common interests that fit within the SERP agenda.

While flexibility about the configuration of field sites is important, they must be willing and be judged able to work as a partner in a SERP Network on a mutually agreeable local version of the SERP agenda. This will require buy-in from both the teaching and the administrative staff. Among the most important factors are

- access of SERP research teams to schools, classrooms, teachers, student records, etc.;
- a sufficiently long-term commitment (and arrangement for continuity if change of leadership occurs) to justify the initial investment;
- released time for teachers to work with research teams, for professional development, and for reflection and interaction with other teachers;
- adherence to research protocols and sampling requirements;
- adoption of SERP assessments and performance measures; and
- effective collection of district, school, classroom, and student data to support evaluation.

Field sites should be committed to promoting the transfer of fruitful findings and applications throughout the school, district, and wider system. The ultimate aim of SERP is to foster widespread improvement, not just change in one school or 10 SERP field sites. This will require replication of promising interventions in the range of environments in which the research-based change might be applied, as a necessary part of the process of bringing the most successful innovations to scale. Field sites engaged in the original research can play an important role in the process of supporting the "travel" of effective practices to new locations.

This contextual emphasis will make possible the kind of follow-through that has seldom characterized education research. For example, understanding how interventions work in classroom settings requires that the research and development be carried out in a pre-determined range of settings and with a variety of students. Understanding the needs of teachers for support in using educational interventions, as well as the characteristics of schools that support or undermine change, also requires that schools be available as sites for investigation. Learning more about the personal and environmental characteristics that distinguish excellent teachers from their less effective peers calls for observation and analysis in situ.

Are there alternatives to the model of a strong central office and dispersed field sites described above? The committee did consider whether a strong SERP center was necessary, given that many of the researchers and practitioners SERP would need to attract are located in dispersed university and school settings. Without a strong center, however, we envision an outcome that would mimic what we see today: a situation in which even the best work is not carried forward, there is little coordination and accumulation of research across sites and centers, the opportunities to coordinate data collection and analysis are routinely missed, and the dissemination of findings is haphazard. Moreover, dispersion of activity across many research loci without a coordinated mechanism for review, assessment of progress, and course correction would make quality control difficult. As a result, the agenda of research centers and individual researchers might be constrained relatively little by the strong program goals of improving educational outcomes.

Similarly, the issues of whether field sites are necessary was considered, with the alternative being one of funding researchers who themselves have made arrangements to work in school settings. But the transaction costs of arranging for that work, for both the researcher and the school, are high, and the projects become highly dependent on personal relationships. The committee concluded that to efficiently undertake work on the scale envisioned and to draw many more researchers and practitioners into such collaborations, much of these costs would need to be borne at an institutional rather than an individual level.

ORGANIZING THE RESEARCH AND DEVELOPMENT PROGRAM

How should the program be organized to effectively bring the resources of the research and development community to bear on the problems of practice? Should it be structured around problems as they are manifest in the world of practice, like improving mathematics performance in urban school districts, or problems as they are defined in the world of scientific research—around sets of issues that share theoretical underpinnings and research paradigms, like the core conceptual components of mathematical proficiency?

Persuasive arguments can be made for each if the goal is to improve student learning. On one hand, current understanding of mathematics learning will serve as a constraint on the potential of a reform effort. The best intentions for improving mathematics performance are unlikely to produce impressive results without an understanding of how children learn mathematics and the nature of the problems that result in failure to learn. If the goal is to advance the effectiveness of the education we provide to students, defining a scientific research program that pushes the boundaries of current understandings would seem to be an essential component.

At the same time, however, those engaged in practice are only too aware that research on learning will make little difference to schools in the absence of effective organizational supports and public policy incentives for change. Because researchers by tradition address questions of learning and instruction, organizational change, and policy separately, it is difficult to build on research to improve practice—where all are at play simultaneously. We have concluded, therefore, that this is not an either/or proposition. Because the organization of knowledge does not map the realities of educational practice, we have designed the SERP research program to be responsive both to the strengths of current scholarship and the complexities of the educational system that we are aiming to improve. We provide an argument for one organizational arrangement, but note that others are possible and may be preferred by those who ultimately are responsible for building a SERP enterprise.

SERP Networks

The first level of organization that we propose is a set of networks broadly defined by fields of research: for example, learning and instruction, schools as organizations, and education policy (see Chapter 4 for further discussion of networks). While each network will be interdisciplinary (e.g., learning and instruction would bring together cognitive scientists, developmental psychologists, education researchers, and discipline experts in reading, science, mathematics, etc.), research traditions and methods are likely to be shared to a much greater extent within these networks than across them.

We use the term "network" to refer to a dispersed community of participants whose work in a broad topic area is actively linked through productive collaborations. The networks will promote synergy across researcher-practitioner teams working on common agendas to extend the boundaries of current understanding in each broadly defined field.

For SERP to achieve the kind of programmatic strength that, for example, the National Cancer Institute did in the 1990s, the networks will need a central organizing intelligence to give coherence and direction to the program. The design plan anchors the planning process for each network in the SERP headquarters; thus, we expect that the network headquarters staff would take a leading role in conceptual framing, strategic planning, and coordination.

Intramural Research

We propose that some network research be conducted at the headquarters as well, and that an effort be made to develop a field site in close proximity to the headquarters. Effective steering of a large-scale program will require a primary commitment to SERP, and obtaining that primary commitment from top researchers to an institution that is not conducting intramural research would be unlikely in our view. The committee considered the National Institutes of Health to be an instructive model in this regard. The intramural research program we envision would be a relatively small share of the SERP portfolio—perhaps 20 percent of the total. In the early years, however, the intramural program might play a considerably larger role in an effort to create program coherence.

The headquarters research group will be well positioned to convene periodic meetings of the teams that make up each network in order discuss the progress of the work and assess the need for revisions, course corrections, or a strengthening of the links between the parts. The challenge of coordination is to maintain a creative tension between coherence and growth of understanding on one hand, and dynamism and innovation on the other. In the interest of the latter goals, we recommend that the scientists and professional experts who staff the headquarters research and development program join the enterprise on a fixed-term basis, renewable upon critical outside review.

Extramural Research

As a network's program begins to take shape, SERP will look increasingly to external teams of researchers and practitioners to carry out a large proportion of the research activities. Team members might be located in one place or, if not, be linked through a SERP web site, virtual communications, and regular face-to-face meetings. Some teams might be nominated by the network leadership; others would be chosen through a competitive process in response to a network request for proposals; selection of yet others might be made in response to field initiated proposals.

The creation of extramural research teams when and as needed is intended to lend the SERP enterprise a high degree of flexibility and malleability, while the coherence and continuity required for a strategic program is served by the presence of a core internal research group. Use of external research teams permits SERP to search methodically for and exploit externally generated ideas and a wide array of expertise. It also enhances the organization's responsiveness to the level and kind of effort needed at any given stage of the research program. While some of the research teams are likely to exist only briefly to do limited or highly specific tasks, others will have long-term involvement in the network.

Cross-Network Coordination

While each of the networks would have a separate research agenda, the work of all networks would be brought together at a second, higher level of organization: the research and development department or unit. It is at this level that advances in knowledge from each of the component networks would be integrated for purposes of improving education. Department management would include a department director and the leadership of each of the networks. One of the functions served by that group would be the active coordination of strands of research that are carried out within a network or that cross networks.

To illustrate, we can imagine a scenario in which a learning and instruction network has been conducting a strand of research on the acquisition of reading skills in language minority children. Simultaneously, the network on schools as organizations has been working with a school district that is undergoing a major reform—perhaps like the decentralization reform in Chicago. The school district decides to introduce a research-based intervention for language minority children and wants to study the effects. Two existing strands of research in two different networks are then very relevant to the study, and the combination of expertise from these two networks will strengthen the research design and study of this new strand.

Strands of research that cross networks would, in our judgment, represent a considerable portion of the SERP portfolio. These strands would be managed in an office of internetwork research and development. The participants in these cross-network strands would continue to have a home in a network, allowing for growth and continued contributions in the area of dominant expertise. But network members might spend much (or little) of their time in a particular period working on internetwork strands. This type of organization would take advantage of the gains to be made by defining problems both from a scientific perspective and from a practice perspective.

Network Field Sites

Each field site will become a partner in one or more of the SERP research networks. As partners in SERP, the field sites will be involved in shaping the network agenda. They may have ideas or interventions that warrant study, or they may want to use the collaboration as a way to become more systematic about reflecting on their practice. They may be committed to closing the performance gap between majority and minority students or to finding better ways to educate children whose home language is not English and see opportunities to advance such goals in the network research program.

The SERP organization will provide several kinds of support for the on-site research program, including outreach and public support, research support, on-site research support, and financial support.

Outreach and Public Support   The SERP director will provide information about the initiative to state political, education, and business leaders on an ongoing basis, to encourage a continuity of policy interest in, and support for, the work going on at the field sites. This will help the school districts directly involved in the initiative command the staying power needed to bring about real learning and change.

Research Support   The research arm of each SERP network will include a multidisciplinary team of senior researchers, senior practitioners, and SERP fellows (midcareer, postdoctoral, and doctoral candidates in education or education-allied fields). When SERP establishes a research relationship with a field site, this team will work with the site practitioners to

- negotiate the specifics of the research program and the terms of the collaboration;
- formulate the specific local version of their joint research agenda;
- develop the research protocol and map its implementation;
- provide instructional materials and protocols;
- provide (or work with the site to develop) needed tools, instrumentation, and data systems;

- provide training/professional development for participating teachers, principals, and others involved; and
- engage in discussion, feedback, formative evaluation, and course corrections through e-mail networks, face-to-face meetings, and summer training institutes.

SETTING R&D PRIORITIES

Who should make the decisions about broad program priorities? As with the organization of research, there are different answers that can be supported with compelling arguments. Identifying knowledge bases and research topics in a field that have potential to advance understanding of effective educational practice will require people with deep knowledge of research in the areas of relevance, as well as people experienced in research methodology (including the complexities of conducting research on educational practice). But while the knowledge base of researchers is critical to identifying and developing a productive program, they are not uniquely qualified to determine which questions, if answered, would be of most benefit to teachers, or most feasible to implement, or which type of educational improvement would have greatest payoff for society. Teachers, administrators, and policy makers will have important and very different contributions to make in these regards.

If we take the area of early reading as an example, on one hand, researchers may be best suited to identifying weakness in the current knowledge base that could productively be addressed through research—like opportunities to better understand the problems of children who do not learn to read even with intensive individualized instruction. A teacher, on the other hand, may point out that existing knowledge cannot be effectively used unless there is an investment in research and development on instructional strategies for working with multiple groups of children in a single classroom who require different levels of instruction. School administrators struggling to put well-prepared reading instructors into classrooms may argue that the most important investment is in effective professional development to give teachers of early reading access to current knowledge on effective instruction. In contrast, a policy maker may favor evaluation of major instructional programs to determine what works and what doesn't.

All these groups have legitimate claims to influencing the education research and development agenda, and none is likely to make an optimal set of choices in isolation. Furthermore, if a SERP enterprise is to have the broad buy-in from the communities that it seeks to involve, those communities must have some voice in the agenda. From the committee's perspective, this suggests a research and development program with priorities that are influenced by a group with varied expertise and commitments. However, the design of the final research program must be reserved to those with deep expertise in research and development who have been informed and influenced by those with deep knowledge of classroom and administrative practice whenever appropriate.

An alternative and very practical answer to the question of who should set priorities is that those who fund the research and development should determine the agenda. In a broad sense, this is of course true. Those who allocate money—whether public or private—must be accountable for that spending. However, successful research and development programs that sustain attention over a substantial time period, whether in the military, in medicine, or in agriculture, leave the program decisions to those with expertise in research and development and maintain accountability for spending at an aggregate level.

There are certainly examples of research and development programs in which funders make program decisions. This is currently the predominant model in education. But it is the committee's view that the rapid change in priorities that comes with each leadership change has contributed to the inability in education to develop sustained and cumulative research programs. In the SERP design, then, the committee proposes that funders maintain broad oversight through their participation in the SERP governing board, where ultimate accountability would reside, but that the details of program development should be entrusted to those whose expertise and ultimate commitment is to the quality and productivity of the research and development program.

Before we consider the governance structure in more detail, we turn to the issue of who the funders might be.

ATTRACTING STABLE FUNDING AND SUPPORT

The possible sources of funding for the SERP enterprise that the committee considered were federal, state, and private. Historically, education research and development has been funded predominantly by the federal government through the Department of Education, the National Science Foundation (NSF), and the National Institute of Child Health and Human Development. Private foundations have also supported education research and development, although on a considerably smaller scale. State governments historically have not participated in the research and development enterprise.

In a marked departure from history, the committee is proposing a SERP research and development institution that is funded significantly (though not exclusively) by the states. The considerations supporting the departure from tradition are three:

1. Decisions about the size and distribution of the investment in research and development in any sector are most efficiently considered as part of the production function for that sector. In considering how much to invest in improving understanding of reading difficulties in young children, for example, the investment should be scaled against the budget for reading instruction and the cost implications of reading difficulties. If reading failure leads to grade repetition or special education placement (or both), the cost of those outcomes is highly relevant to considerations of investment in preventing them. Similarly, an investment in research and development aimed at improving the learning opportunities for reading teachers should take into account the size of the budget spent for professional development of teachers, as well as the expected cost implications of improving teacher performance. Because delivery of education services and control of the education budget are largely the responsibility of the states, the states are the logical investors in research and development.

The case for research and development in education as a federal activity is perhaps strongest in regard to the "public goods" characteristics of the activity: The products of research and development in one state can benefit other states as well, creating a potential "free rider" problem. While this might support a case for federal responsibility for research and development, in our view the better alternative is a cooperative agreement among states. The federal government paid less than 9 percent of the cost of elementary and secondary education in 2001, and much of that was devoted to Title I, special education, child nutrition programs, and Head Start (U.S. Department of Education, 2001b). When appropriations for K-12 education research and development are considered at the federal level, they are scaled against the relatively small share of the budget devoted to K-12 education.

At the state level, in contrast, education represents a major priority—about a third of total state general expenditures (U.S. Department of Education, 2001a:Table 31). While the budget allocation varies somewhat with fiscal circumstances and competing priorities, the size of the education budget is relatively stable because states are providing the education services at costs that change relatively little from year to year. Decisions about research and development can most rationally be made as the share of those education expenditures to be devoted to improving education services.

Importantly, because the budget for delivery of education services is relatively stable, embedding R&D in that budget will enhance the prospects for stability that are critical to SERP effectiveness. Funding needs to be stable enough over time to allow for continuity in the research program, as well as confidence and commitment among those who would be recruited to the enterprise. Neither federal nor foundation funding for education research and development has been characterized by long-term commitments or program stability. In the case of the federal government, previous efforts to establish a large-scale federal education research and development institution with a mission much like that of SERP have fallen victim to ambivalence in Congress regarding the federal role in education and to a consequent instability in funding. The committee commissioned a review of that history by Emerson Elliott, a long-time federal career employee who occupied positions from 1957 to 2000 that placed him in the center of this history.[1] We summarize Elliott's central messages in Appendix A.

---

[1]Elliott's positions included four stints as acting director of the education research function, as well as appointment as the first commissioner of education statistics in 1992.

2. The "ownership" of the SERP enterprise suggested by the funding structure should enhance the prospects for productive alliances between those involved in research and development and those involved in delivery of education. The practitioners, schools, and school systems that SERP seeks to bring into partnership, as well as the education decisions that SERP seeks to influence, are responsive to a state and local governance structure. The prospects for success will be greatly enhanced, in our view, if SERP in a sense "belongs" to those who operate within that governance structure. That ownership also provides the most direct tie to the SERP agenda, ensuring that the work of the organization is indeed responsive to the needs of practice.

3. The funding structure needs to bring *substantial new revenue* to education research and development. From the outset, SERP will require some sizable infrastructure investments up front. The ambitiousness of the start-up, as well as the speed with which the institution builds, will depend on the commitment of funds. The committee does not expect that in the current financial environment states will be able to commit substantial new resources. But an agreement to invest in research and development some years down the road when the basic infrastructure is put in place and proof of concept has been demonstrated may be sufficient to give private foundations, and perhaps the U.S. Congress, assurance that a short-term commitment of funds is likely to create an institution that is viable in the long term.

CREATING AN INTERSTATE COMPACT

The idea of creating an interstate compact is not new. The Education Commission of the States was formed in just this way. In 1964 James Bryant Conant, educator, scientist, diplomat, and former president of Harvard University, proposed a compact of states as a mechanism for strengthening education policy and policy making at the state level. The compact, he believed, would allow the states to effectively communicate and cooperate and would serve as a counterbalance to the enlarged federal role in education ushered in by the GI Bill, the National Defense Education Act, and the Great Society legislation. Conant saw the compact not as a way to make state policy more uniform but as a way for states to learn from initiatives in other states so that their own decisions might be better informed.

A draft of the interstate compact that Conant envisioned was endorsed by representatives from all 50 states and the U.S. territories at a meeting in Kansas City in 1965. By the time the functional arm of the compact—the Education Commission of the States—held its first meeting in June 1966, 36 states had formally joined the compact, and it was ratified by Congress. All remaining states joined the compact in later years.

While the Education Commission of the States provides a model for the development of a state compact, the mission and governance of SERP would be different, and we envision the two organizations as entirely independent. The compact we envision for SERP would provide participating states with authority to nominate some members for the governing board and for the agenda-setting advisory board. In this way, states would maintain broad oversight and influence. The compact should be clear in its details, however, that scientific and programmatic decisions would be left to the authority of the SERP director, protected from direct influence by members of the compact.

It would also provide member states with privileged access to SERP workshops, conferences, and materials. In the start-up years when the compact is being formed, SERP would seek short-term funding from existing sources (such as foundations). But eventually states would be expected to contribute a very small portion of their education budget to SERP.[2] Having states committed financially would increase the probability of access to field sites and data systems and help provide continuity in the research program. It would also guarantee the relevance of the program.

To ensure that the SERP program was indeed responsive to the needs of member states, arrangements could be made to pay part of their "dues" for the support of the organizational infrastructure (e.g., data collection, quality control, communications) and part to individual networks or projects on a discretionary basis. In this way states with common problems—like large

---

[2]If all states joined an interstate compact to which they contributed just one-quarter of 1 percent of their elementary and secondary education budgets, the total funds available for R&D would fall in the neighborhood of 800 million dollars per year.

numbers of language minority students, or severe teacher short-ages—could effectively combine their resources to support efforts of particular importance to them.

To develop the capacity of the states to operate a compact that can promote the long-term effectiveness of SERP, resources (human and financial) will need to be set aside from the start for that purpose. Some of the required investments in research and development may take years to bear fruit. Staying the course with long-term investments poses a challenge to policy makers whose success is measured by short-term outcomes. If they are to see a new role for themselves in steering the education research and development enterprise in directions that are productive in the long run, support for playing that role will be required. More broadly, SERP must attend to building state capabilities to participate in helping to frame, carry out, use, and evaluate research and development.

A FLEXIBLE FUNDING STRUCTURE

While we propose that core, stable funding for the SERP program would eventually flow from a compact among the states, we think the vitality of the SERP program, and the reach of the SERP infrastructure, will be enhanced if the organization is receptive to participation from a variety of other sources as well. We see two alternative models. The first would invite participation from federal agencies, foundations, regional compacts, and businesses at the level of specific research initiatives or specific SERP field sites. This would provide the flexibility for them to simultaneously enhance the impact of their own efforts and the SERP program. Support from the National Science Foundation for a SERP study of implementation of model science curricula, for example, would provide the opportunity for NSF to fund independent field site testing and evaluation. The results of that work would further both the NSF and the SERP agendas.

A second alternative would incorporate the first, but it would also allow for a longer-term commitment from the federal government agencies or private foundations to the annual SERP budget that would earn them a place on the governing board of the organization. To the extent that the potential partners see the success of a SERP infrastructure as enhancing their own goals and their ability to carry out their own work, the more extensive participation provided for in this second option would be desirable.

· ·

THE SERP GOVERNANCE STRUCTURE

Success of the SERP enterprise will require strong leadership. To attract that leadership, the director of SERP needs to be invested with broad authority and accountability. Above all else, attracting a highly competent director to SERP will require minimizing political influence on that appointment. The interests of the states, other funders, and the schools and school districts that participate in SERP will be best served, in our judgment, if the quality and effectiveness of the institution are the primary criteria on which leadership is judged.

The director would serve at the pleasure of the SERP governing board, being hired (and fired) by this board. It will therefore be necessary for the governing board itself to be composed of individuals who can be entrusted to promote and protect the quality and efficacy of the SERP work: individuals who command public respect across party lines for their service in the public interest.

The membership and size of the governing board will be decided by those who fund SERP, and will no doubt need to be adjusted as SERP grows and prospers. The committee's image of the governing board is one of perhaps a dozen members, who might be drawn from the ranks of former governors known for their commitment to education in their states, industry leaders with a personal involvement in educational improvement, presidents or provosts of institutions of higher education, and those who have served as effective public spokespersons for the importance of educational improvement.

Fiduciary responsibility for the institution would rest with the governing board. Approval of general program direction, budgets, large initiatives, and oversight of quality in personnel and program would be its responsibilities as well. While the board would approve creation and cessation of research and development networks and the allocation of financial resources across networks, that ultimate responsibility for agenda setting in SERP must reside with the director. The director would be responsible for setting policy, planning, managing, and coordinating programs. The director's decisions will be informed and guided by his or her key appointees, including the leadership of the research and development networks. Since the networks are themselves collaborations of researchers and practitioners, those communities will influence decision making indirectly.

The committee thinks that two advisory boards are also important to bringing an external perspective from the scientific and practice communities to the director. The first is the scientific advisory board described above, a board with responsibility for oversight of the research design and the peer review process. We envision this board as a group of paid agents of the institution appointed for their methodological expertise, serving on a part-time, fixed-term basis. A second agenda-setting advisory board would bring perspectives to the director on the pressing problems of policy and practice that should be considered in setting the SERP agenda. Unlike the governing board members, who would be prominent figures, these advisory board members would consist of individuals whose everyday experiences keep them in close touch with the problems of classroom practice and policy making: teachers, principals, curriculum directors, superintendents, and legislators. These, too, are envisioned as paid, part-time, fixed-term positions.

· ·

SERP ORGANIZATIONAL STRUCTURE

Ultimately, decisions about the structure of SERP will be made by its funding partners and by its original governing and management team. We envision a substantial gestation period, during which the number of initiatives grows and the SERP program matures. Here we lay out a potential organizational arrangement that can serve as a point of departure for discussions of a SERP launch. We have not tried to anticipate or resolve every issue of organizational design that an entity of this complexity can expect to encounter. Rather, we have tried to identify a limited number of key features. Like parents caring for a newborn that they hope to nurture to a vital and productive adulthood, we can make some choices to encourage healthy development right now. But many decisions will be best made only after observing and responding to growth as it occurs.

In the design we envision, SERP functions are carried out in four operational units that report to the SERP director (see Figure 3.1). These are research and development, quality assurance, communication and public liaison, and management, budget, and administration. We refer to operational units and offices as a means of both identifying critical functions that a SERP organization must carry out and indicating lines of authority and responsibility that will promote a healthy organizational dynamic. The major challenge of the SERP management team, however, will be one of creating a flexible and dynamic organization. This will require primary attention to the functions to be performed rather than the offices that perform them, as well as to the links that keep the functions productively and responsively connected rather than the boundaries that distinguish them.

1. A *research and development* unit would coordinate the research and development networks and the internetwork initiatives. The number of networks should be small at the start—no

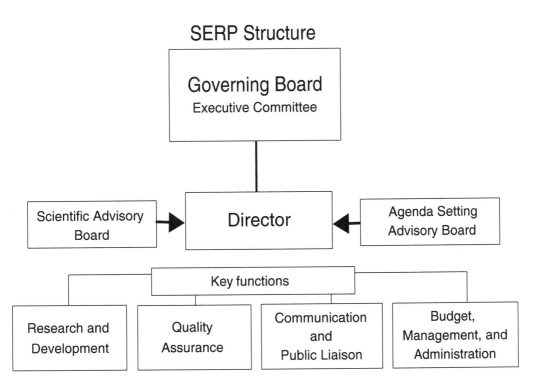

FIGURE 3.1 SERP structure.

more than three—but that number might grow over time. Each network would include intramural and extramural research and development efforts and would partner with one or more field sites (Figure 3.2). The SERP commitment to partnership would find immediate and visible expression if each network were led by a duo of one practitioner and one researcher. Ideally they would be chosen for their ability to address the network's hub question and their skill at leading research teams whose members are diverse in professional background and expertise. Above all, they must be open to the possibilities and ready for the challenges of collaborative work. These leaders should be very talented people at the height of their careers. They will oversee the network's overall research plan, nurture productive interactions and collaboration among the parts, and provide intellectual coherence to the whole. They will also be responsible for seeing that the network provides carefully developed research protocols and the other tools and instruments needed for work in the field. It is crucial that the leaders be closely connected

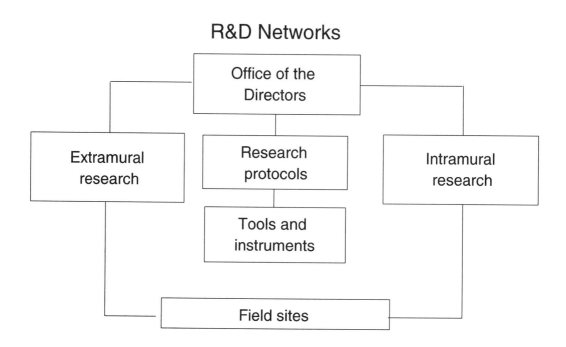

FIGURE 3.2 R&D networks.

with the central functions of SERP and also intimately familiar with the field sites where SERP is operating.

An office of internetwork initiatives would house research that draws on multiple networks and would carry out the same functions of research management as the networks. Field sites would join one or more networks, providing the context for carrying out much of the research on practice.

The *research and development* unit would house five other functions as well. The other functions are: planning and evaluation, communications, research services, fellowships and appointments, and data collection (Figure 3.3). Planning and evaluation will operate like an internal consulting group, consolidating knowledge about instrumentation, research protocols, and evaluation of research and development projects. Ultimate responsibility for each of these tasks would lie elsewhere: in the networks and the quality assurance office. However, developing capacity, particularly in the early stages, may be facilitated by providing expert support.

Although there will be an operational unit responsible for communications and public liaison, we nonetheless propose a communications research and development office housed in the research unit. Effective communication will be the key link between the research and development program and improving student learning. A central message of the report *How People Learn: Brain, Mind, Experience, and School* (National Research Council, 2000) is the importance of the organization of knowledge. It is in that organization that meaning, and a foundation for informed response, is created. How knowledge can be organized to maximize learning and support for knowledge utilization must itself be the subject of study if SERP is to have an impact on student and teacher learning. Where that study can best be undertaken is a somewhat difficult question. Communications has not been an area of high status for researchers. If SERP is to attract high-quality researchers to this critical study, it will have to set out to elevate that work. We propose that this be done in part by infusing communications questions throughout the research program. When teacher learning is the subject of study, communicating findings effectively to teachers and schools of education should be on the agenda. When policy incentives are the topic, communicating effectively with policy makers should be a subject of study. We do not propose that the communications functions themselves be carried out by the

Research and Development Department

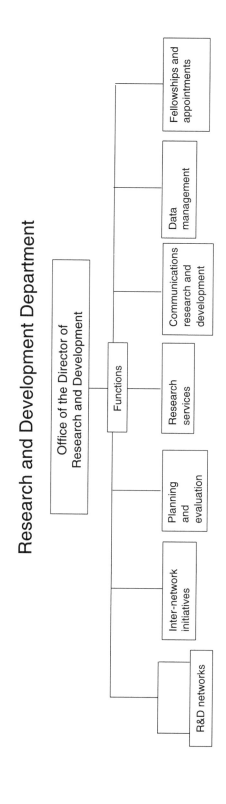

FIGURE 3.3 Research and Development Department.

networks, but that the research to support communications be done here.

Research services would house a variety of functions to facilitate the process of working in field settings. It would handle terms and conditions of participation, contracts and agreements, negotiations for time release and job protection, and human subject protections. It would also handle library and information functions, and other services common across research and development initiatives.

Since the SERP proposal entails a substantial increase in capacity to carry out research in field settings, our design assigns the task of capacity building to a fellowships and appointments office that would recruit and provide learning opportunities for postdoctoral fellows and arrange for visiting positions for university professors and for teachers. There are many Ph.D.s in science, mathematics, and engineering who are not employed by universities, and whose expertise might productively be channeled to education research (National Research Council, 2002a). SERP would provide an opportunity that does not now exist for training in education research. This function is housed in the research and development unit of the organization to ensure that capacity is developed where it is needed to support the programs.

Each of the research efforts would presumably involve data collection, but we propose a separate data management office that would build a longitudinal dataset that incorporates a common set of measures for all participating schools. The key constituency for this office will be the networks themselves. This office, like each of the networks, may undergo dramatic change through the gestation period. If the states in the compact wish to invest in a common data collection system, for example, they could decide to undertake their existing, regular data collection and reporting in a common format and to have that data aggregated at SERP headquarters. This would greatly expand the size and function of the data office, giving states a far greater capacity to understand and guide the education system.

Those responsible for each of the functions described would report to a director of research and development, who would hold major responsibility for coordinating the efforts. The director would monitor if and when projects in different networks overlapped and required coordination, or when work in one network should inform that of another. This individual would also be responsible for monitoring the work of other education research institutions, actively looking for opportunities to leverage and coordinate existing efforts.

2. A *communications and public liaison* unit would provide a bi-directional link between the SERP program and schools and teachers across the country. The vision of SERP as a place for teachers, administrators, policy makers, and researchers to turn for well-organized information and access to the current knowledge base will be realized only if a substantial investment is made in that function.

Beyond making relevant knowledge usable, a SERP organization must attend to getting usable knowledge used. Accumulation and sense-making, in other words, are not all that is required. Effective communication and support for knowledge utilization—including navigation through the knowledge base, technical assistance, and connections to others inside and outside the SERP organization—are essential.

For example, SERP needs to be a place to turn when a fifth grade mathematics teacher is looking to understand and solve her students' problems learning long division. We see it as a place where a superintendent can go to get performance data on curricula that have been studied in SERP field sites or information about the in-service preparation requirements that accompanied successful interventions. Exploitation of new technologies will give SERP a platform to engage the research, practice, and policy communities in dialogue about what the research findings mean, or the kinds of experiences teachers are having as they implement a particular curriculum, or the latest performance data in districts that have implemented one of the SERP-sponsored programs.

This office will itself conduct—or commission from outside sources—research and program evaluation aimed at ascertaining the effectiveness of communications with the diverse audiences that SERP intends to reach.

Close coordination between the research and development networks and the communications unit will be critical and will warrant the creation of positions in both with responsibility for that coordination. The appointment of an associate director for communications who reports to the SERP director would ensure that the function of communications is elevated.

The functions of the communications and public liaison unit would include handling public information, news and media, technical assistance to schools, and online information. Over a period of gestation, we can imagine the efforts of this office expanding greatly, creating, for example, online communities of teachers who are working with a particular curriculum, topic, or problem. This office could also provide support to the SERP director in undertaking capacity building for those involved in the state compact.

3. The *quality assurance* unit would have two major functions: outside review and SERP program evaluation. The two functions are quite distinct. The outside, peer review process would provide assurances regarding the quality of the SERP work. Scientific standards would be central to this evaluation.

The SERP program evaluation function, in contrast, would focus on the value added by the SERP endeavor. The charge of this office from the outset would require the development of measures of SERP program effectiveness. These would probably involve evaluative feedback from the SERP user community and funders, as well as efforts to measure the impact of SERP on education policy and practice. This last goal without question will be a major challenge, but one the committee thinks warrants a serious effort from the start. The education enterprise is huge. A research and development effort aimed at improving its productivity, if it were eventually allocated just 1 percent of the education budget, would itself be huge. As in the private sector, the decision about how much to allocate should depend on the contribution that research and development makes—the productivity of the investment.[3] Unless an effort is made to develop measures of that productivity, SERP could become a set of bureaucratic commitments rather than a vibrant research and development enterprise.

4. Finally, a *management, budget, and administration* unit would house financial, personnel, and facilities management functions.

---

[3]More precisely, the allocation should depend on the *expected* productivity of the investment based in part on past returns.

SUMMARY

Our proposed design will create, in our judgment, the conditions for a newborn SERP to thrive. Its essential features can be summarized as follows:

- A governance structure that ensures accountability, broad representation of the views of the variety of education stakeholders, a long-term commitment to central goals, and the scientific integrity, quality, and usefulness of the program.
- High-quality leadership of the organization chosen for substantive expertise and a commitment to the mission of the institution.
- Research and development networks designed as collaborations of researchers, practitioners, and policy makers, linked to field sites that allow for the study of practice and policy.
- An organization of the research and development program designed to simultaneously push the boundaries of academic disciplines in areas of promise for improving student learning and to bring together multiple fields of research relevant to problems of practice to improve understanding and decision making.
- Monitoring of quality assurance and program impact by those not directly involved in the conduct of the program.
- The development of capacity building within the institution to carry out the type of program SERP seeks to undertake.
- Elevating communications to a high-priority function that will include research and development.

As SERP grows, we would expect the organizational structure to be reshaped and refined, its areas of expansion responding to the demand of the field and the successes and failures along the way.

4 SERP Networks: Who Would Come and What Would They Do?

I n Chapter 3 we sketched a picture of each of the SERP organizational parts. In this chapter, we turn to animation of the SERP core: the research and development networks. What incentives would bring researchers, practitioners, and school systems to collaborate in the networks? And once they joined the efforts, what type of work would they do? Finally, we consider the incentives for those engaged in the delivery of education to make use of what SERP would offer.

CREATING NETWORK PARTNERSHIPS

The nature of the collaboration contemplated for SERP is different in quality and scope from any currently in place in education. The committee has found the teaching hospital a useful metaphor for the envisioned collaborative relationships: the functions of practice and research would in good part be located in the same site (SERP field sites), professional preparation of both practitioners and researchers would be merged with high-level research activity, and links with university research departments would be strong.

WHO WOULD COME?

There are many examples of existing partnerships between researchers and practitioners, including the cases described in Chapter 2. When scaled against the size of the K-12 education system, however, the number is dwarfed by the need. Even more importantly, these partnerships generally require Herculean efforts on the part of individuals and are very difficult to sustain when those individuals move on. How can SERP create a set of incentives for participation by both researchers and practitioners that makes collaboration more commonplace and that facilitates the maintenance of those collaborations in a sustainable fashion?

BRINGING RESEARCHERS TO SERP

To create an organization with the capacity to attract high-quality researchers, we need to know what motivates the decisions of researchers' regarding the work they pursue. The committee's hypothesis is that researchers decisions can be roughly characterized as balancing five considerations, although the weight given to each varies tremendously across individuals. The five are reputation, career opportunity, intellectual stimulation, income, and the ability to make civic contributions through their work to the public good. While an individual researcher may value one of these highly and another very little, we think each of the five is important to some researchers. The more participation in SERP can advance—or at least not jeopardize—these goals, the more successful the institution will be at attracting outstanding researchers.

Reputation and *career opportunity* are closely linked. Both are promoted when researchers produce high-quality, publishable work. SERP would promote productivity and quality in research in its program in several ways, among them:

- By building a high-quality, well-maintained, longitudinal database.

High-quality, longitudinal datasets are the workhorses of empirical research. They allow tests of hypotheses regarding causal relationships that cross-sectional data cannot support. And they allow correlations over time to be observed that support new hypotheses and theory building. They also fuel a great number of publications. The National Education Longitudinal Study (NELS), conducted by the National Center for Education Statistics, is a case in point. A large body of research has been spawned in the years since the first follow-up in 1990 to the initial data collection in 1988.

In order to carry out the program of research envisioned for SERP, longitudinal data collection that allows for empirical investigation of the long-term effects of curricular interventions, instructional strategies, organizational environment, and policy choices will be required. In this sense, the needs of the research program overlap directly with the professional needs of researchers.

To meet both needs will require that data collection be a high priority and be adequately funded by the institution from the start.

- By supporting the capacity for rigorous research design.

The overall quality of research produced through SERP will determine whether affiliation with the institution enhances or detracts from a researcher's reputation. Providing institutional standards and support to engage in high-quality work can therefore enhance both the quality of the individual's work and the draw of the institution in the community of researchers. SERP would support quality by creating and maintaining high standards for research design through the scientific review board and peer review processes described in Chapter 3.

Quality research is likely to enhance one's reputation more if it is noticed. By building a coherent program of research, we would expect individual contributions to carry more significance because they are part of a body of work that together supports a set of understandings and provides a foundation for decision making. In this sense, the more effective the SERP effort to steer the research and development program in productive directions, the greater will be the draw of the institution.

Many researchers see their greatest career opportunities in university positions. For this reason, affiliation with SERP must be compatible with university commitments. The proposed SERP structure, with most of the research and development being carried out in dispersed field sites where researchers and practitioners partner, allows for a simultaneous commitment to a university and to SERP research. In addition, SERP would need to work actively with universities to obtain permissions for researchers who come to SERP headquarters to obtain multiyear, fixed-term leaves of absence.

We would expect *intellectual stimulation* to be a natural by-product of SERP. We would argue that stimulation is likely to be highest in two situations: when people from the same field come together to push the boundaries of understanding in that field, and when people from different fields work together on a problem, allowing for multiple paradigms and models to generate new understandings and ideas. SERP would expand the opportunities for both types of stimulation substantially. The research agendas of the networks would keep research teams in close contact and collaboration in order to advance the knowledge base. And SERP would create a venue for a type of interdisciplinary work on education issues that has been relatively rare because education departments in universities have generally not been successful at attracting scholars from other disciplines. But perhaps the most powerful lever SERP would wield to increase the intellectual options for researchers would come from the opportunities that SERP is specifically designed to create and nurture: allowing for disciplinary researchers to work closely with research-oriented practitioners. Negotiating the relationships with expert practitioners that lead to real collaborative research is not easy, and yet anyone who has benefited from such a relationship recognizes that it is highly productive and enormously stimulating.

Researchers who value making a *civic contribution* through their work may be thwarted by the logistical difficulty of doing so. The lack of an infrastructure that links research and practice makes it difficult for education researchers to contribute to the education system. *Education Week* recently published a story about a Harvard education researcher, Richard Murnane, who decided to spend a sabbatical year offering his help to the local school district. While Murnane's effort eventually resulted in an ongoing connection with the schools through which he is helping train practitioners to effectively use data about their students, getting there was not easy. Neither Murnane nor the schools knew at the outset what, if anything, he could do to be helpful. His determination kept him in a situation that was at first quite awkward. By facilitating links between researchers and schools, SERP would allow for those interested in making a civic contribution to do so without having to leap such a high barrier to search for a place in which to be useful individually.

Attracting researchers to problems of education—like all other research problems—will be greatly facilitated if there are *financial rewards* for doing so. There are clear precedents in military, space, and medical research. The relatively meager funding of education research and the instability of the federal commitment of funds for education research over the years have not created a strong pull on intellectual resources to the problems of education. If SERP operates with a relatively stable, sizable budget as described in Chapter 3, there will be a financial incentive for researchers to turn their attention to the problems of educational practice that could become quite powerful as the commitments of states grow.

ATTRACTING PRACTITIONERS TO SERP

What would motivate teachers to participate in collaborative research? We hypothesize rather different incentives in the case of teachers. Because the rewards of the profession are quite different, what is likely to be required in order to compete for a teacher's time commitment will be different as well. While the financial rewards of teaching are not as great as those in research, what teaching does provide is an opportunity to engage with students in a meaningful, sometimes life-shaping, way. It gives one an opportunity to open new worlds, and new opportunities, to students. SERP, we believe, will be attractive to teachers if the SERP work allows them to do their jobs more successfully and to influence the lives of their students more positively. SERP will provide an opportunity for teachers in the sense that the knowledge from research will be brought to bear in context and on the problems of practice. We envision SERP as providing professional development opportunities for teachers and summer stipends to attend SERP seminars and workshops.

Teaching can also be attractive for the job stability it provides and for the predictability of the schedule. But precisely those characteristics can pose a challenge to attracting teachers to SERP. The rigidity of a teacher's schedule does not typically allow for other commitments during a school year, nor for job security or seniority in the case of an extended absence. For SERP to attract teachers, institutional arrangements will need to be made with schools to provide for either a teacher's extended leave without penalty or a reduced workload to allow for participation in a research project during a school year. The negotiation of these arrangements through the office of research services should create opportunities for teachers that are now lacking.

As with researchers, teachers will vary tremendously in their drives for intellectual stimulation and to make a contribution to their profession writ large. Teachers who seek venues for these purposes currently have few options. Teachers and administrators lead activity-driven lives; they are rewarded for working long hours and being endlessly "available." They are not rewarded for reflection on their practice. Moreover, much of their work is done in isolation from others in the profession. As several of the cases in Chapter 2 suggest, practitioners who want to empirically test teaching approaches or interventions are often left to find their own path to the world of research through unmarked territory. Certainly not every teacher is interested in working with research teams. But for those who are, SERP will provide a venue that does not now exist.

Finally, much of the SERP work would be designed to learn from teaching practice, so the knowledge that teachers bring will be actively employed and valued. For teachers who do look to research, it can be quite frustrating that what is available often does not address the complexity of the problems they face. The opportunity to influence the research agenda is likely to be an important draw for this group.

ATTRACTING FIELD SITES

Why would schools, school districts, or states agree to serve as field sites for SERP research? The primary answer, in our view, is that education leaders at all three levels have a desire—whether motivated by civic contribution, reputation, career opportunity, or accountability measures—to do a better job of educating students. If SERP is successful in its early years at linking research and practice to improve student learning outcomes, we think that attracting new field sites will be facilitated by the expectation of continued success. It may be more of a challenge, however, in the start-up period before proof of concept has been demonstrated.

For this reason, early efforts to establish field sites should target schools and districts that have demonstrated interests in engaging in research and development efforts. School districts in Boston, Chicago, Pittsburgh, and Providence, for example, currently work with researchers. While drawing on exciting opportunities is not likely to produce a representative sample of schools or students, it should provide the foundation for success early on that will create the possibility of a representative sample of field sites further down the road.

The benefits of the SERP research will be available to all schools in all states that join the SERP compact. It therefore stands to reason that the costs of the field site research should be borne primarily by the organization rather than the participating schools. To encourage field site participation and an efficient distribution of costs, we propose that SERP funds be used to buy out teacher time and cover other new costs imposed by the research. When expenditures substitute for those made routinely by a participating site (e.g., an investment in data collection), costs should be shared so that the school is neither taxed nor subsidized by involvement with SERP.

WHAT WOULD THEY DO?

If SERP is successful at attracting researchers, practitioners, and field sites, what will they do when they join a research and development network? The answer to that question will be determined by those who are given leadership responsibility in the new organization. Below we provide our vision of what that leadership might do.

The committee is proposing the inauguration of three networks during the start-up years, although others may eventually be added. We recommend that a learning and instruction network be initiated at the very start because the relative maturity of research in the cognitive and developmental sciences holds promise for real improvement in how teachers are prepared and what they do in the classroom. A second network on schools as organizations would, we think, be a critical companion to the learning and instruction network because the organizational environment of the school creates the conditions and incentives required to support and sustain instructional change. We anticipate that as work progresses during the start-up years, each network would develop five to eight related strands of work that speak to its hub question, employing the full panoply of research methods (experimental design, longitudinal studies, observational techniques, formative and summative evaluations, etc.) in an iterative process that produces ever more refined knowledge.

We propose a third network to house research and development on issues that profoundly influence both instruction and organization management: education policy. This network would embrace research on issues like accountability testing, class/school size, education finance, school choice, desegregation, and other policy issues that create the incentives and environment to which teachers and schools respond. How quickly a third network is put in place will depend in large part on the funds available to launch the SERP enterprise.

• •

AN ILLUSTRATIVE AGENDA FOR A SERP NETWORK ON LEARNING AND INSTRUCTION

To make the case for the value of a SERP research and development program more concretely, an expert panel of practitioners and researchers was convened by the National Research Council to complement the work of our Committee. Its task was to design an illustrative agenda for one network that would simulate, in a sense, the role of the agenda-setting advisory board and the leadership of a learning and instruction network. We selected this network from among those proposed because the National Academies have in recent years produced important syntheses of the research literature on human learning (National Research Council, 1999) and on assessment of learning (National Research Council, 2001), as well as discipline-specific syntheses in reading and in mathematics (National Research Council, 1998, 2001). These and other explorations of the knowledge base on learning and instruction (National Institute on Child Health and Human Development, 2000; RAND, 2002a, 2002b) provided a rich foundation on which our effort could build.

This focus is not intended to suggest preeminence of the learning and instruction network. In our judgment, the organizational and implementation issues associated with educational change are also absolutely central to SERP's mission. Efforts to improve learning and instruction, the motivation and engagement of students and teachers, and the quality of curricula, assessments, and instructional materials cannot succeed unless they are attentive to the variety of organizational and institutional contexts in which instruction occurs. Indeed, in our view, it is in combination with the work of other networks that the research and development on learning and instruction will have maximum likelihood of influencing practice.

GENERATING A CONCEPTUAL FRAMEWORK

Because the intended focus of the SERP program of research and development is educational practice, the conceptual framework proposed by the learning and instruction panel begins not with the questions posed by any research discipline, but with the questions that define teaching practice. The point of presenting this conceptual framework here, before we get to the specifics of the agenda proposed for the area of early mathematics, is to demonstrate how broadly one needs to be able to think about educational research and improvement—how many different perspectives and sources of knowledge are needed to think productively about even a single, specific, focused research problem. SERP's competitive advantage is precisely that it can bring together the array of researchers and practitioners who can keep these many different perspectives in play simultaneously.

We can view classroom instruction as organized around a set of core questions that apply no matter what the subject:

- What do we want students to know or be able to do?
- What are the typical understandings and preconceptions students hold on this topic at the outset?
- What is the expected progression of understanding and skill mastery, and what are the predictable points of difficulty or hurdles that must be overcome?
- What instructional interventions can move students along a path from their initial understandings and skills to the desired outcome (curricula, instructional activities, etc.)?
- What general and discipline-specific norms and practices best comprise and support student learning?
- And finally, how can the individual student's progress be monitored and the student be engaged in

the instructional activities that she or he needs to take the next step toward increased understanding and skill?

Whether explicitly or implicitly, by design or by default, teachers answer the above questions in the course of their teaching practice. In doing so, teachers (like professionals in other fields) draw on standards of practice, professional preparation, background knowledge, tradition, and personal inclinations and intuitions. A program of research and development can improve the answers to those questions by providing a solid knowledge base to support both teaching practice and professional preparation, as well as by expanding the instructional and assessment tools available to teachers.

The questions that define educational practice can be informed by several very different fields of research and knowledge:

- *What students should know or be able to do* in an area is informed (but not fully determined) by disciplinary expertise. It requires an understanding of the core concepts around which the disciplinary knowledge is organized, characteristic methods of reasoning and problem solving, and language and patterns of discourse. What to teach becomes not only a matter of the information and skills considered important but also of helping the student to build the conceptual framework that transforms or helps to organize information into understandings.

- *Knowledge of common student conceptions of a topic and the expected progression of student thinking* requires careful research on the typical trajectory of understanding. In part this research attempts to identify the nature and limits of children's changing cognitive abilities with age and instruction. And in part it attempts to uncover common understandings that can either support learning (the ability to halve or double relatively easily in mathematics) or undermine it (the belief that heat and temperature are the same thing). Research findings demonstrate the remarkable resilience of students' everyday understandings even after instruction to the contrary (and often to the great surprise of teachers). This highlights the importance of a carefully designed research program to inform and support practice. Research of this sort is often done by cognitive scientists and education researchers, although the knowledge may emerge from the experience of expert teachers and the observation of exemplary practice.

- *Educative experiences* intended to move students along a learning path constitute the core of what we consider to be "instruction." These experiences are ultimately created by the teacher, but teachers usually draw on materials generated by curriculum developers or (less often) researchers. Instructional programs involve assumptions about the contributors to skill development, knowledge acquisition, and conceptual change that should themselves be a research agenda, and the effectiveness of the instructional approach is a matter for empirical testing.

- *General and discipline-specific norms and practices that support student learning.* Learning takes place in classrooms that are themselves communities. Every community is distinguished by norms for work and interactions, ranging from when and how people collaborate to how they speak with one another. Some of those norms are general—rooted in the understanding of schools in a democratic society; others are specific—what it means to do mathematics differs from what it means to do literary analysis or chemistry or history. How individual norms contribute to or undermine student learning, and how this differs by community, are empirical questions that draw on sociological and psychological understandings, as well as on a rigorous evaluation of classroom practices.

- *Assessing* the current level of an individual student's understanding is itself an interdisciplinary undertaking because it requires an understanding of both what constitutes learning and how to measure it. To be useful in the learning process, the assessment must be tied to instructional responses. Assessment, then, requires that the knowledge relevant to each of the above questions be incorporated into the design and testing of specific instruments.

The knowledge bases described above must be incorporated into teacher education opportunities, instructional programs, curriculum materials, and other tools that facilitate the work of the teacher. The learning and instruction network must therefore be concerned both with shoring up the knowledge base on each of the questions above *and* on incorporating that knowledge into education programs, tools, and teaching protocols. Practice is not embodied solely in the tools and protocols of the trade, however. Rather, these work in tandem with both the knowledge and skill of the practitioner.

TEACHER KNOWLEDGE AND LEARNING

Teacher knowledge and skill matters a great deal in student learning. Ferguson (1991) analyzed data from 900 Texas school districts and found that teacher licensing exam scores, masters degrees, and experience accounted for over 40 percent of the variance in students' reading and mathematics achievement scores after controlling for socioeconomic status. Other studies suggest a similarly powerful effect (Ferguson and Ladd, 1996; Strauss and Sawyer, 1986). Yet despite its importance, the research base on teacher learning is relatively undeveloped; the grasp of the content of the teacher knowledge that produces achievement is shallow.

The questions above that we argue define teaching practice apply just as aptly to teacher learning as to student learning. For teachers, however, we have a good start on the first question: "What do we want the teacher to know and be able to do?" The answer is defined by the questions that frame teaching practice. We want teachers to understand the learning process of the student well enough to assess and guide it; the content well enough to select appropriate instructional materials, guide the pace and direction of instruction, and flexibly respond to student questions and thoughts; the curriculum materials well enough to use them as a means to an end rather than as the end itself; the norms and practices that constitute effective practice well enough to create a supportive learning environment in the classroom; and assessments well enough to interpret the outcomes and respond appropriately.

What is not well defined are the forms of knowledge a teacher must master in order to reach that end and what levels of mastery are needed. What mathematics must a teacher know, and what pedagogical knowledge is required, to make and implement appropriate decisions about the best instructional steps to develop student thinking about rational number, for example? Although these questions are central to effective practice, little research has been done to provide answers.

Moreover, learning is as complex an undertaking when the teacher is the target as it is when the student is the target. Teachers' conceptions of learning and instruction, of student thinking and age-specific capabilities, and of the subject matter often diverge considerably from research-based findings (National Research Council, 2000; Palincsar and Herrenkohl, 2002; Palincsar et al., 1989). These existing conceptions must be understood and engaged. And experiences that bring about conceptual change for the teacher must be designed and effectively deployed for learning to occur.

More complex still than creating conceptual change is the relationship between a teacher's knowledge and instructional practice. Practice requires knowing what elements of the knowledge base are relevant in a specific situation and what characteristics define the situation itself. This is what is meant by "conditionalized knowledge." A comparison to medicine is illuminating. Understanding well how the human body functions and malfunctions does not ensure that a medical student confronted with a patient will know which avenues to explore in response to a description of symptoms, or which features of the patient are particularly worthy of note. A medical student who has finished course work is not permitted to practice alone without first having extensive experience in observing the knowledge used in the context of practice.

Much that teachers need to know cannot be learned apart from practice, just as learning to ride a bike requires experience with the thing that is being learned (Polyanyi, 1967). This raises several questions for inquiry: Under what conditions can teachers best learn while engaged in practice? What knowledge and skill must teachers acquire at the beginning of their careers? What knowledge and skill is best acquired once they enter the profession? What organizational, material, and human resources are necessary to support and sustain teacher learning over time?

The conceptual framework adopted by the learning and instruction panel, then, is defined by the questions that teachers must answer to effectively educate their students, and the questions teacher-educators must answer to effectively prepare teachers for practice. The framework can be applied no matter what the subject matter to be taught.

A STRATEGIC AGENDA

In the long run, providing research-based knowledge to support answers to the above questions for every subject taught in schools is a desirable end—just as one expects the treatment of any ailment by a physician to be based on research-based knowledge (amplified by craft knowledge). Yet the reality of the limited resources devoted to education research and the existing capacity to conduct that research suggest the need for focus on a limited set of subjects in order to ensure that work can be carried through all stages necessary for usability. As a knowledge base is consolidated in some areas, attention can be devoted to new subject areas.

The panel chose three areas for focus: mathematics, science, and reading. The rationale for its choices, as well as the full agenda in each of the domains, appears in a companion report, *Learning and Instruction: A SERP Research Agenda* (National Research Council, 2003b). To develop a strategic agenda, the committee sought to identify subject areas in each domain that fall into two categories: (1) areas in which considerable progress has already been made in answering some of the important questions of instruction. Additional work that builds on that success can be expected to contribute to improvements in practice in the relatively near term. Work on whole number, early reading, and physics falls into this category. (2) subjects characterized by fundamental gaps in the knowledge required to inform instruction. Algebra, elementary and middle school science, and reading comprehension fall into this category. While the first group takes advantage of existing opportunities, the second begins with pressing problems of practice.

In each area, the panel considered the relative, and in some cases unique, advantage of the SERP infrastructure for supporting research and development. In this chapter we discuss just one of the focal areas from the full panel report as an example: elementary mathematics.

ELEMENTARY MATHEMATICS

Investment in recent decades by federal agencies and private foundations has produced a wealth of knowledge on the development of mathematical understanding, as well as numerous curricula that incorporate that knowledge. As a result, elementary mathematics is ripe for productive investments in making that knowledge usable and used widely by schools. The committee had the benefit of drawing on a recent synthesis of research on elementary mathematics (National Research Council, 2001) and on the work of a RAND study group that produced a mathematics research agenda (RAND, 2002b).

What Do We Want Children to Know or Be Able to Do?

A recent consensus report at the National Research Council (2001) shows that U.S. students fare poorly in international comparisons of mathematics achievement. They show weak understanding of basic mathematical concepts, and although they can perform straightforward computational procedures, they are notably weak in applying mathematical skills to solve even simple problems. These results have generally been attributed to the shallow and diffuse treatment of topics in elementary mathematics relative to that in other countries, as well as an instructional emphasis on repeated practice with paper and pencil skills in arithmetic (National Research Council, 2001).

This report also provides an argument for what elementary schoolchildren should know and be able to do in mathematics that draws on a solid research base in cognitive psychology and mathematics education. The consensus includes mastery of procedures but places far more emphasis on understanding when and how to apply those procedures. The latter is rooted in a deeper understanding of mathematical concepts, and a facility with mathematical reasoning. The report identifies five intertwining strands that constitute mathematical proficiency (National Research Council, 2001):

- *Conceptual understanding*—comprehension of mathematical concepts, operations, and relations;
- *Procedural fluency*—skill in carrying out procedures flexibly, accurately, efficiently, and appropriately;
- *Strategic competence*—ability to formulate, represent, and solve mathematical problems;
- *Adaptive reasoning*—capacity for logical thought, reflection, explanation, and justification;

- *Productive disposition*—habitual inclination to see mathematics as sensible, useful, and worthwhile, coupled with a belief in diligence and one's own efficacy.

The instructional issues, then, involve the means to achieving this more ambitious goal of mathematical proficiency.

Progression of Understanding

Research has uncovered an awareness of number in infants shortly after birth. The ability to represent number and the development of informal strategies to solve number problems develops in the child over time. Many studies have explored how preschoolers and young schoolchildren understand basic number concepts and begin operating with number informally well before formal instruction begins.

Children's understanding progresses from a global notion of a little or a lot to the ability to perform mental calculations with specific quantities (Griffin and Case, 1997). Initially, the quantities children can work with are small, and their methods are intuitive and concrete. In the early elementary grades, they proceed to methods that are more general (less problem dependent) and more abstract. Children display this progression from concrete to abstract in operations first with single-digit numbers, then with multidigit numbers. Importantly for instruction, the extent and the pace of development depend on experiences that support and extend the emerging abilities.

Researchers have identified two issues in early mathematics learning that pose considerable challenges for instruction:

1. Differences in individual experiences result in some children—primarily those from economically disadvantaged backgrounds—entering kindergarten as much as two years behind their peers in the development of number concepts (Griffin and Case, 1997; see Chapter 1).
2. Children's informal mathematical reasoning and emergent strategy development can serve as a powerful foundation for mathematics instruction. However, instruction that does not explore, build on, or connect with children's informal reasoning processes and approaches can have undesirable consequences. Children

can learn to use more formal algorithms, but are likely to apply them rigidly and sometimes inappropriately (see Box 4.1). Mathematical proficiency is lost because procedural fluency is divorced from the mastery of concepts and mathematical reasoning that give the procedures power.

Curriculum Development

Past investments in research and development have produced curricular interventions to address each of the two problems raised above. A well-developed and promising research base on the Number Worlds curriculum suggests that well-planned activities designed to put each step required in mastering the concept of quantity securely in place can allow disadvantaged students to catch up to their more advantaged peers right at the start of formal schooling. The curriculum has a

• •

BOX 4.1   Buggy Algorithms

When students attempt to apply conventional algorithms without conceptually grasping why and how the algorithm works, "bugs" are sometimes introduced. For example, teachers have long wrestled with the difficulties that second and third graders frequently have with multidigit subtraction in problems, such as

```
  51
 −14
_____
```

A common error is

```
  51
 −14
_____
  43
```

The subtraction procedure above is a classic case: Children subtract "up" when subtracting "down"—tried first—is not possible. Here, students would try to subtract 4 from 1 and, seeing that they could not do this, would subtract 1 from 4 instead. These "buggy algorithms" are often both resilient and persistent. Consider how reasonable the above procedure is: in addition problems which look similar, children can add up or down and get a correct result either way:

```
  51
 +14
_____
  65
```

Bugs often remain undetected when teachers do not see the highly regular pattern in students' errors, responding to them more as though they were random miscalculations.

companion assessment tool (the Number Knowledge Test) to help the teacher monitor and guide instruction. If results in controlled trials (see Chapter 1) could be attained in schools across the country that serve disadvantaged populations, this would represent a major success with respect to narrowing the achievement gap—a long-standing national goal that has proven difficult to realize.

With respect to the second concern, research done in the 1990s investigated the effects on student achievement of instruction that builds on informal understandings and emphasizes mathematical concepts and reasoning. Cobb et al.'s Problem Centered Mathematics project (Wood and Sellers, 1997) and Cognitively Guided Instruction (CGI) in problem solving and conceptual understanding (Carpenter et al., 1996) both reported positive effects. With support from the National Science Foundation (NSF), several full-scale elementary mathematics curricula with embedded assessments have been developed, directed at supporting deeper conceptual understanding of mathematics concepts and building on children's informal knowledge of mathematics to provide a more flexible foundation for supporting problem solving. Three curricula developed separately take somewhat different approaches to achieving those goals: the Everyday Mathematics curriculum, the Investigations in Number, Data and Space curriculum, and the Math Trailblazers curriculum (Education Development Center, Inc., 2001).

While theories of learning help to identify problems these curricula have been designed to address, the curricula themselves involve theories of instruction that must be tested. Do their efforts to provide more contextual learning opportunities that link students' informal thinking to mathematical problem solving produce students with stronger mathematics skills overall, or are there trade-offs among the component skills? Do they perform as well for students who excel in mathematics as for students who struggle?

All three curricula show positive gains in student achievement in implementation studies in which the developers collect data on program effects. While such findings are encouraging, they must be viewed with a critical eye, both because those providing the assessment have a vested interest in the outcome and because the methodology employed does not allow for direct attribution of the results to the program. Third-party evaluations using comparison groups have been done, but none of these has involved random assignment (the condition that maximizes confidence in attributing results to the intervention). Nor do these studies measure either fidelity of implementation of the reform curriculum for the experimental group or the specific program features of the alternative used with the control group (see, for example, Fuson et al., 2000).

From the perspective of practice, these are important omissions. To make informed curriculum decisions, teachers and school administrators need to know what type of implementation of a specific curriculum produces what results, compared with what alternatives. Ideally, the reform curricula would be compared with traditional curricula that are highly rated or widely used (or both) in order to advance the knowledge base for practice. Yet to provide the information that is most useful to practice is a major undertaking. These questions are answerable, but research carefully designed to provide the answers will take a substantial, long-term investment.

Assessment

The curricula described above have embedded assessments that allow teachers to track student learning. As previously mentioned, a key feature of the Number Worlds curriculum is the Number Knowledge Test that allows teachers to closely link instructional activities for children to the assessment results. How well other curricula link assessment and instruction is an issue worthy of investigation.

A separate issue is the assessment over time of the five strands that constitute mathematical proficiency. The last decade has seen the emergence of a spate of new tests and measures. No consensus has emerged, however, on critical measures. While there are some standard and widely used assessment tools to appraise young children's emergent reading and language skills and competence, no such tools are used on any comparable basis in primary mathematics.

This type of assessment will be required to evaluate the effectiveness of a particular curriculum and to make comparisons across curricula. For the most part, we lack sophisticated methods for tracking student learning over time or for examining the contribution of any particular instructional interventions, whether large or small, on students' learning. A research project that focused on mathematics teaching and learning might begin by developing such tools.

Teacher Knowledge

Little is known about what it might take for teachers to use particular instructional approaches effectively, a necessary element of taking any particular approach to scale. The challenges can be substantial. The curricula mentioned above introduce major changes in approach to teaching mathematics, and effective implementation will require that teachers change their view of mathematics teaching and learning dramatically. In Everyday Mathematics, for example, teachers are expected to introduce topics that will be revisited later in the curriculum. Complete mastery is not expected with the first introduction. This has created some confusion for teachers, who are often unclear about when mastery is sufficient to move on to the next topic (Fuson et al., 2000). All of the curricula encourage building on students' own strategies for problem solving and supporting engagement through dialogue about the benefits of alternative strategies. The change required on the part of the teacher to relinquish control of *the answer* in favor of a dialogue among students, where it has been studied, has proven difficult to master (Palincsar et al., 1989). The risks of change must be considered as well: if a teacher does turn control of the discussion over to students but is not prepared to guide that discussion productively, precious little learning may go on. Critical to the effectiveness of efforts to implement such curricula on a large scale, then, is that there be adequate teacher preparation and ongoing support for an entirely different approach to teaching. This is clearly an important area for further study.

One clue regarding teacher knowledge requirements can be found in research pursued for the most part separately from the work on student learning and the design of curriculum approaches, tools, and materials discussed above. Investigations of teachers' knowledge reveal that although teachers can, for the most part, "do" the mathematics themselves, they often are unable to explain why procedures work, distinguish different interpretations of particular operations, or use a model to closely map the meaning of a concept or a procedure. For example, teachers may be able to use concrete materials to verify that the answer to the subtraction problem in Box 4.1 is 37 and not 43. They can operate in the world of base ten blocks[1] to solve $51 - 14$ but may not be able to use base ten blocks to demonstrate the meaning of each step of the conventional (or other) algorithm.

Similarly, teachers may be able to compute using familiar standard algorithms but not be able to recognize, interpret, or evaluate the mathematical quality of an alternative algorithm. They may not be able to ascertain whether a nonconventional method generalizes or to compare the relative merits and disadvantages of different algorithms (for example, their transparency, efficiency, compactness, or the extent to which they are either error-prone or likely to avert a calculation error). Over and over, evidence reveals that knowing mathematics for oneself (i.e., to function as a mathematically competent adult) is insufficient knowledge for teaching the subject. In the domain of early number, studies suggest that most teachers' own knowledge is solid, but that their understanding of conceptual foundations is uneven.

Following this work, some materials for use in teachers' professional development have been developed.[2] Modules and other curriculum materials contain focused work aimed at helping teachers learn the sort of mathematical knowledge of whole numbers and operations that is needed for teaching. As with the curricula developed for students' learning discussed above, developers of teacher learning materials provide some evidence of teachers' learning of mathematics for teaching, but they have studied less the role of this learning in the teacher's subsequent instructional practice and effectiveness.

Still less is known about what teacher developers themselves need to know to support teachers' learning and how their professional learning might be supported. The demand for skilled leaders who can teach teachers is growing, but the field, though highly remunerative, is unregulated and all too often typified by inadequately trained instructors and badly designed

---

[1] Base ten blocks are a common material used to model place value concepts and operations that rely centrally on place value. The materials consist of a unit cube, a ten-stick built of 10 cubes, a flat square built of 100 cubes or 10 ten-sticks, and a block composed of 1,000 cubes, or 10 flats, or 100 ten-sticks.

[2] See, for example, work by Schifter and her colleagues at Education Development Center, Developing Mathematics Instruction (Schifter et al., 1999).

delivery methods. Scaling up materials that can support teachers' learning of mathematics for teaching will require worrying about the knowledge requirements of those who will guide and support the teachers.

The SERP Agenda

Given the current state of practice and knowledge about learning and teaching of early number, then, what might a SERP program of research and development seek to do? How might it build on what currently exists and begin to extend and fill gaps in what is known and done, with the ultimate goal of more reliably and productively building evidence-based instructional practice? In other words, how could work be planned and carried out that would extend what is known and take that to scale in U.S. schools?

The proposed agenda is comprised of three major initiatives. The first focuses on developing assessments to measure student knowledge, a second evaluates promising curricula and the effects of their particular design features on student outcomes, and a third focuses on the teacher knowledge requirements to comfortably and effectively use curricula that are built on research-based findings regarding student learning.

Initiative I: Developing Early Mathematics Assessments. Quality assessments depend on three things: (1) clarity about the competencies that the assessment should measure; (2) tasks and observations that effectively capture those competencies; and (3) appropriate qualitative and quantitative techniques to give interpretive power to the test results. Clarity about the competencies to be measured requires a theoretical understanding (that is empirically supported) of mathematics learning. Unlike many other areas of the curriculum, early mathematics has the theoretical and conceptual models, as well as supporting empirical data, on which to build quality assessments. Substantial work has already been done to specify critical concepts and skills within this domain, providing assessment developers with resources on which to draw in drafting the elements of a measurement strategy.

Even with a strong foundation on which to build in early mathematics, much work remains in designing and testing assessment items to ensure that inferences can be accurately drawn about student knowledge and competencies. And this work must be carefully crafted for the specific purpose and use of the assessment, for example, formative assessment for use in the classroom to assist learning; summative assessment for use at the classroom, school, or district level to determine student attainment levels; or assessment for purposes of program evaluation.

Formative assessments are essentially diagnostic. They can, for example, provide feedback to the teacher on a student's mastery of a particular skill or concept or on whether individual students need more time and practice before moving on to new material. Summative assessments are also used in the classroom, but they come at the end of a unit. They give a teacher feedback on how well the students have mastered and brought together the set of concepts and skills taught in the unit. These may be helpful to the teacher in redesigning instruction for the next year, providing valuable data on students' strengths and weaknesses that can inform instruction at the next level. School- or district-level assessments have more general policy purposes, most commonly to determine attainment levels for groups of students in order to evaluate the effectiveness of an instructional program; to monitor attainment by racial, ethnic, or disability category; and in some cases to hold schools accountable for the performance of their students.

Currently the different types of assessment are loosely connected at best. Tensions are introduced when strong instructional programs and accountability assessments are at odds. Better aligning assessments—and tying all assessments firmly to the theoretical and empirical knowledge base—are widely regarded as critical to improving learning outcomes. The construction of such a system represents a major research, development, and implementation agenda that would require the kind of stability, longevity, and support that SERP intends as its hallmark.

The above work should be pursued as a collaborative effort involving teachers, content area specialists, cognitive scientists, and psychometricians. The effort could use as a departure point well-established standards in mathematics (e.g., National Council of Teachers of Mathematics), standards-based curricular resources, and rigorous research on content learning to identify and define what students should know in early mathematics, how they might be expected to show what they know, and how to appropriately interpret student performance. In the case of formative assessment, this extends to an understanding of the implications of what the evidence suggests for subsequent instruction. In the case of summative assessment, this means understanding the implications of student performance for mastery of core concepts and principles and the growth of this mastery over time.

While there are several possible approaches to developing such a system of student assessments in early mathematics, one obvious place to begin is with a review of the assessment materials in existing widely used and exemplary curricular programs for formative and summative assessments, commercial testing programs, and state and national tests for policy making and accountability. These can be reviewed in light of cognitive theories of mathematical understanding, including empirical data regarding the validity of specific assessments. Research needs to focus on evidence of the effectiveness of specific assessments for capturing the range of student knowledge and proficiency for particular mathematical constructs and operations. A related line of inquiry would focus on issues of assessment scoring and reliability, particularly ease of scoring, consistency of scoring within and across individuals, and consistency of interpretation of the results relative to the underlying cognitive constructs.

The development of assessments in early mathematics should be closely tied to complementary initiatives in the areas of teacher knowledge and curriculum effectiveness. Thus a strand of research focused on implementation issues should address the set of questions critical to successful use of quality assessments:

- What teacher knowledge is necessary to support effective use of assessments in their instructional practice? These include teacher understanding of the assessments and their purpose, as well as practical considerations of the time to administer, score, and interpret results.
- What forms of technology support are needed to assist teachers in the administration, scoring, and interpretation of a range of standards-based and theory-based assessments?

- How and to what extent does the process of implementing curriculum-based and standards-based assessments lead to changes in teachers' instructional practices, and how do these changes affect student learning outcomes? This investigation should focus both on changes in the near term and the stability of changes in the long term.

High-quality evidence that permits practitioners, researchers, and policy makers to ask and answer comparative questions will be critical to making the SERP research and development usable in practice.

Initiative II: Teacher Knowledge. To take advantage of existing investments in research and development in elementary mathematics will require further work regarding teacher learning and knowledge requirements and the supports that allow teachers to use these curricula comfortably and effectively. This research should begin with a clear articulation of the principles and assumptions about student learning that the curriculum incorporates, comparing these to carefully solicited understandings of teachers. Learning experiences should be designed to address the points of divergence and tested for their power to change teacher conceptions.

Further research should test the effectiveness of different components of professional development on both teacher learning and the learning of their students. The relative benefits of teacher guides, videotaped cases, and opportunities to pose questions and receive support should be tested, as well as the timing effect (before instruction begins, during instruction, etc.) for different teacher learning opportunities.

Initiative III: Curriculum Evaluation. The identification (and further development) of a set of approaches to the teaching of number and operations that vary on distinct and theoretically important dimensions would permit careful comparisons of how particular instructional regimes impact students' learning. Programs and approaches already developed, such as Number Worlds, Cognitively Guided Instruction, the three NSF-supported curricula mentioned above, and well-regarded and widely used traditional curricula would form the initial core, but analysis would permit such a core set to be complemented with other theoretically and practically important alternatives.

Many of the evaluations of the curricula set out to answer the question, "Does the curriculum improve student achievement?" While this is an important question—and of particular interest to those who market a curriculum—the questions of importance for long-term improvements in practice are why, for whom, and compared with what? Number Worlds shows very promising results for disadvantaged children; Everyday Mathematics does as well. How, and for whom, do those outcomes differ? Are there trade-offs in the competencies children gain from each? Does the context in which they work best differ? Each of the three NSF elementary mathematics curricula takes a somewhat different approach to instruction. How are those differences reflected in outcomes for students? Does one better address the needs of low- or high-achieving students? What are their respective organizational and implementation requirements? Are there lessons in the outcomes that could be used to improve any of the curricula or to combine features not now found in a single curriculum?

An analysis of existing candidate materials could illuminate important differences, and strategic selections could be made. The implementation, adaptation, and use of these different approaches could be followed over time, attending to instructional practice, students' opportunities to learn, and implementation issues. In addition, based on what is known about teachers' knowledge of whole number and operations for teaching, as well as about teacher learning, systematic variations could be designed to support the implementation of these different instructional approaches. For example, in one set of schools, a teacher specialist model might be deployed, and, in others, teachers might engage in a closely focused study of practice (instruction, student learning, mathematical tasks), co-planning and analyzing lessons across the year. In still others, teachers might be provided with both incentives to spend time planning and adequate teacher guides.

The work could be conducted in carefully controlled, longitudinal studies carried out in SERP field sites. A SERP organization like that described in Chapter 3 would be well positioned to carry out such work. Because it would have mutually beneficial relationships established with a number of field sites and data collection efforts in those sites already under way, taking on a controlled experimental study of alternative curricula would be a far less daunting task than it would be for researchers working independently. Moreover, the concern for undertaking research that is maximally useful to educational practice and the ability to design and conduct—or oversee the conduct of—that research will be combined in a single organization. This is a situation that does not now exist.

The research initiatives described above provide a glimpse through a single window of a large-scale SERP research and development enterprise. The companion report provides a more extensive agenda, but even that is limited to the learning and instruction network. Perhaps the greatest benefit of the proposed SERP organization is that programs of research on schools as organizations and on education policy will be developed alongside that of learning and instruction. Yet, even within the confines of the early mathematics agenda considered here, distinguishing features of SERP are apparent. This includes an effort to define a program of research that focuses on the problems of practice, strategically building on strengths in the existing knowledge base and shoring up its weakness.

WOULD SERP CHANGE PRACTICE?

Even the highest quality SERP research and development will make a difference only if it is used in practice. What incentives will teachers, schools, districts, and states have to make use of the SERP work?

As we mentioned in the opening chapter, the current climate in which schools are being held accountable for student performance creates some motivation to search for the means to improvement. While this may lubricate the wheels of change, large-scale accountability will not be a sufficient motivator. It is, by its nature, low-level accountability; it generally attends to gross measures of skill performance. The SERP program, in contrast, is targeted at improving learning for understanding. This more difficult change in instruction will require more powerful motivators. These, in the committee's view, are (a) solid evidence that change will bring clear benefits in student performance and (b) support for implementing the change in real classroom environments.

Regarding the first, we have proposed an investment at the outset in measures of program outcome for all of the SERP work. As the case of the Cognitive Tutor Algebra I in Oklahoma suggests (see Chapter 2), the resistance to making a change often lies in the doubt that the new program will in fact be better, as well as the risk that it may be worse. Careful efforts to document student gains will, we think, serve as a significant inducement for teachers and schools to change their practices. In the proposed research and development agenda, the effort to measure impact permeates every strand of research. Furthermore, the organizational design assigns to those responsible for quality assurance the task of measuring the impact of SERP research and development. In doing their job, an additional source of pressure will be placed on the research and development program to define clearly the expected program outcomes, so that impact data can be compiled as programs are implemented. These data will help inform school districts and states about the potential improvements associated with change. Together we expect these efforts to provide a powerful motivation for change.

But motivation is not itself enough, either for the higher-level change sought by SERP or the lower-level change encouraged through accountability standards. Motivated teachers still must have the support to change their practice. The idea of attending seriously to what it takes to use research-based practices at the school level runs throughout the envisioned SERP program. Carrying out much of the work in a range of classroom settings will allow the problems of classroom use to themselves be a subject of study and an issue for development and program design. Indeed, in the Oklahoma case, the combination of evidence of success and support from the school district and the program developer to change curriculum resulted in *all* teachers preferring the new program, making continued controlled experimentation difficult. It is the unique combination of attention to carefully measured outcomes and attention to the requirements for classroom use that leads the committee to be convinced that SERP can make the kind of change possible that has been so difficult to achieve in the past.

5 Charting a Course of Action

The organizational design and illustrative research examples we have proposed for the Strategic Education Research Partnership (SERP) are shaped by our key objectives: building deep and reciprocal connections between practice and research; producing a research program noted for its quality, and the accumulation of useful and usable knowledge; building talent for this collaborative work in the research and practice communities; and having impact on what teachers do, how schools operate, and—foremost—on student learning.

Our search for ways to promote research and development of high quality that focuses on important issues of educational practice has led to the design of a program that is intended to influence many parts of the education system: the development of curricula, materials, and technology that support improved practice; strengthening the curriculum and expanding the research roles of colleges of education; improving professional development; organizational and system change to support improved practice; and, not least, the creation of mechanisms and incentives for teachers and researchers to work together to improve student learning.

Much of our work here in developing a prototype organization design and research agenda is intended to illustrate the potential of a SERP enterprise to change significantly the nature of education research and development and its interaction with educational practice. To take our illustrative effort one step further, the committee attempts to breathe life into the design by envisioning these interactions in progress a decade into the future. The vision, elaborated in Box 5.1, is meant to suggest the role of SERP both in maintaining a productive focus on a program of research and development, and in responding flexibly

BOX 5.1 A Scenario: SERP A Decade After Launch

What might SERP become under circumstances of adequate funding, good administration early in its process, and success in attracting high-caliber personnel? We would expect three to five networks to exist by the end of a decade, each working on several strands of research. We look here only at the learning and instruction network (LIN). Needless to say, any of the specifics might well be substituted by others, but this hypothetical exercise is meant to give a sense of the envisioned development, scope, and organization of SERP activities.

The SERP-LIN intramural research team consists of 15 senior scholars, a mix of eminent researchers and recognized, reflective practitioners, who provide leadership to the entire package of activities and carry out a part of the SERP-LIN research themselves. This team is responsible for the following:

- agenda setting within the broad priorities set by the Director and approved by the governing board;
- soliciting partnerships with field sites and with external research teams;
- managing the interfaces between the research being done by SERP internally and externally;
- implementing and overseeing the SERP fellows programs designed to nurture and educate the new generation of educational practitioners and researchers (i.e., postdoctoral to midcareer researchers learning how to conduct research in ways compatible with the complexities of practice, as well as reflective practitioners learning about research and its use).

As part of its research effort, the SERP-LIN research team is pursuing a research agenda with a particular site, a large urban school district. In collaboration with the leadership of that district, a site-specific research agenda has been identified that maps onto the parts of the larger network agenda of greatest interest to these schools. The school district has expressed the following priorities:

- to focus on improving student learning in the domain of middle school reading comprehension across the various domains, including English, science, and history;
- to link more closely to a large nearby teacher education program so that preservice teachers are prepared specifically for the curriculum, standards, and student body present in the district;
- to link professional development programs more organically to the preservice preparation and to involve both accomplished practitioners and teacher education faculty in overseeing it; and
- to improve capabilities in the school district central office in using information that derives from tracking student progress.

The following research agenda, negotiated with the field site, is tightly associated with these priorities:

1. *Evaluation of instructional approaches to support reading comprehension in the early grades.* Since reading comprehension in middle school builds on proficiencies developed in earlier years, this site will participate in field testing of new early reading curricula developed in several extramural research programs that integrate instruction in decoding, listening comprehension, vocabulary development, and early writing. The curricula differ in (a) the time spent on explicit vocabulary instruction, (b) the time spent in oral reading in the classroom, and (c) whether explicit attention is given to metacognitive strategy development. SERP agrees to prepare the teachers and provide support during implementation. The district agrees to randomly assign teachers to the different curricula and to randomly assign students in a particular school and grade to teachers' classrooms. The school will record the data needed by the research team, and SERP will analyze those data.

2. *Instruction in teaching reading comprehension for middle school practitioners.* Recent research and development regarding reading comprehension within disciplines has led to the development of teaching protocols to support comprehension. The SERP headquarters research team has monitored the research findings and is interested in conducting research on the teacher requirements for effectively using the instructional protocols. SERP and the schools have negotiated a mutually beneficial agenda in which professional development in reading comprehension instruction for middle school teachers is conducted under experimental conditions. In the first two years, the SERP-LIN team will design the research to test

hypotheses about approaches to supporting conceptual change in teachers, the hours of professional development required, and the benefits of doing professional development before versus spaced throughout the period of implementation. In years three and four, the hypotheses will be formally tested. The training will be funded through a SERP project grant, and the school district will pay for the teachers' time spent in training through a state subsidy program for professional development. The school district agrees that teachers in each discipline will be randomly assigned to the different training approaches. The school will collect data on student achievement in reading comprehension throughout.

3. Teacher education faculty in the nearby university are being involved in the research activities so they become more familiar with the district's needs and goals; highly experienced teachers from the district are given release time to coteach methods courses and to help supervise the student teachers from the program. Changes in the teacher education curriculum are being monitored by researchers, and a comprehensive assessment of preservice teacher knowledge implemented three years ago is being systematically administered to all teacher education students and newly hired teachers on a yearly basis, so that individual progress can be monitored. It is hoped that ultimately a task force will take on a more extensive revision of the teacher-education curriculum.

4. A teacher-career approach to professional development (including induction year support, involvement in regular peer learning groups for three years, and assumption of responsibilities as a coach and ultimately master teacher later on) is being implemented and evaluated.

5. Having established a system for tracking individual student progress for the district, the research team is now exploring various methods for giving teachers and administrators access to student progress records. Various alternatives are being explored, including providing teachers with hand-held assessment systems to encourage regular assessment and automatic recording of the data for uploading, providing specialists who incorporate reviewing student progress into the regular professional development sessions, and providing an interactive web site for the data so that teachers can explore their own students' records independently. After a period of initial exploration and surveying responses to prototype systems, one of these systems will be more widely implemented and evaluated.

This research undertaking by the learning and instruction network is clearly large in scope and varied in the range of activities needed to accomplish its aims. In fact, the many topics go beyond the expertise available at SERP headquarters. Because none of the intramural research team members is expert in the field of middle school reading, a number of experts in reading comprehension were commissioned early on to work on the definition and assessment of reading comprehension in that age range. To build on several facets of their work, the collaboration of a team of reading comprehension researchers from a university in the Midwest was then solicited. That team, the first extramural research team in SERP-LIN, was given resources to develop and pilot test instructional protocols for reading comprehension. The SERP home team also established a relationship with a network of Catholic parochial schools in their state, so that the new research team would be able to engage in pilot testing and observation with a student body similar to that of the urban school district SERP-LIN is already collaborating with.

Because SERP-LIN's collaborating urban district serves many students who are speakers of Vietnamese, Khmer, Cantonese, and Gujarati, it was deemed necessary to develop some particular expertise about Asian immigrant populations and Asian-language speakers. Accordingly, SERP issued a request for proposals for a collaborating research team. A team of anthropologists and linguists from several universities in California was selected from the half dozen respondents. They in turn established a California research program focused on school achievement and second language learning among Asian immigrant students, which qualified to become an affiliate of SERP-LIN. They obtained funding from the University of California system to initiate a research project to document the academic trajectories of highly successful Asian immigrant students attending state universities, as well as Asian immigrant high school graduates who have been somewhat less successful academically on state university campuses. They are now extending their work downward by tracking the younger siblings of the university attendees, who are still in middle or high school or who have dropped out of school.

As the work focused on Asian immigrant students started to generate publications, SERP received unsolicited proposals from other teams around the country arguing that the achievement gap between European-

American and Hispanic or black students deserved focused attention from SERP, despite the fact that such issues were not particularly salient in the district with which SERP-LIN was working. None of the unsolicited proposals was deemed of sufficient quality to merit adoption by SERP.

Because of the importance of the issue, however, SERP research staff consequently established a list of priorities for research on the achievement gap and invited submission of formal proposals from teams that incorporated both researchers and practitioners and that specified the site for the work. Ultimately, a well-established network of smaller school districts in which the achievement gap has been well documented for some years, teamed with a consortium of research partners, won the competition and was established as an official field site in the SERP undertaking. Among the commitments made by the field site was to collect data on black and Hispanic students that would parallel in some respects that being collected by the group focused on Asian immigrant students, and that instructional protocols developed and tested by SERP-LIN would be the basis for any particular focus on middle school reading or high school science in the networked districts.

Other school district-research team partnerships that had been working on the issue of the achievement gap petitioned to be affiliated with SERP as well. After SERP headquarters carefully reviewed their leadership, demographics, commitment to research-based practice, and researcher quality, two of these were offered affiliate status (which offers participation in the SERP accumulation, vetting, and communication activities). Three others were turned down.

Regular exchange among the four major locations where SERP work is being done is maintained by virtue of monthly web-based discussions for all participants, regular conference calls among the principle investigators and major project leaders at all sites, and face-to-face meetings every six months.

---

to the emerging needs and interests of the variety of participants whom it seeks to bring together.

GETTING TO LAUNCH

What will it take to get from where we are today to a well-functioning SERP? We begin by grappling with the very difficult task of estimating the initial costs of building a SERP. Placing a price tag on start-up is challenging because so many of the decisions made by the funding partners will have order-of-magnitude effects on program costs. As a hypothetical exercise, the committee commissioned an estimate of costs given a very rough and quite conservative set of assumptions about the pace of start-up, the number of networks (i.e., two), and the size of projects within networks. The reasons for the conservatism are two: first, the capacity for the work we envision will need to be created, and, second, the commitment of resources to research and development is likely to take some years to build. The illustrative SERP research agenda, described in Chapter 4 and spelled out fully in a companion report (National Research Council, 2003b), envisions a breadth and scale of work that would have a genuine influence on practice. To do the proposed work well will require joining research and product development designed to improve learning and teaching to research and development designed to improve schools and systems. Doing such linked work is complex. It requires the mobilization of many talents, much effort, and much more money than has ever been invested in educational research and development. How quickly the capacity and resources to do that work can be built, however, will be determined through negotiations among the variety of decision makers who must commit resources to the effort.

We assume that during that period, the scale of work would build toward, but not yet come close to, that envisioned in the agenda. Over a seven-year period of program development, the costs for the start-up program are estimated at about $500 million (see Appendix B for estimates and assumptions).[1] Early efforts, as the panel report indicates, could build on areas in which substantial progress has already been made in order to support productive outcomes in the near term. In the long run, as capacity to undertake the coherent but very broad work envisioned is built, we would expect the investment to grow substantially.

How much of that investment will be new, how much can come from pools made available to support state efforts to introduce and evaluate research-based practices through the No Child Left Behind legislation, and how much can come from redirecting resources currently allocated to activities that can be carried out more effectively in the context of a SERP organization, is not yet known. While the size of the investment envisioned may be daunting at the start, given the meager funds traditionally allocated for education research and development and current fiscal strains, even 0.5 to 1 percent of a year's budget for elementary and secondary education would yield two to four times the amount estimated for the first seven years. For

---

[1]Committee member David Cohen comments: This report calls for an ambitious program to improve students' learning by improving knowledge about learning, teaching, and schooling. The proposed work is badly needed, and if done well, would yield many benefits. In today's fiscal crisis, it is easy to worry that frankness about the costs of such an endeavor could defeat efforts to get it started. One reason that previous efforts of this sort have done so poorly is that great hopes were saddled with trivial budgets. It would be a pity if this sad history were to be repeated.

any sector of the economy, this is a relatively small rate of investment in research and development.

Getting to the point of undertaking research and development will require an initial effort to build the coalition that will eventually support SERP. Our proposal for the launch phase draws from the history of the Education Commission of the States. To take Conant's idea of a state compact (see Chapter 3) and make it a reality, two foundations (Carnegie and Ford) funded the creation of the compact. Their contributions allowed for support of Terry Sanford, former governor of North Carolina, to work with the leadership of the states to form the compact, as well as for staff to write the terms of the compact and to begin making organizational arrangements. States joined with a commitment to contribute to the funding of Education Commission of the States further down the road, when it was a functioning organization that would provide benefits to its membership. But the initial decision to join the compact was not tied to an immediate allocation of funds. We see the separation of a commitment to the idea and the allocation of state funds to be equally important today, particularly given the immediate strain on state budgets.

While Sanford worked to create the state compact, support was garnered at the same time from the U.S. Congress, which ratified the creation of the compact. Similarly, the SERP launch should involve an active effort to engage the federal government and its education research agencies in the formation of the institution.

In the committee's view, support from foundations for the launch of SERP will be critical to its success. The investment we envision will be substantial, although it is loaded toward later years, when we would expect state contributions to phase in. Still, launch would likely require the commitment of multiple foundations and the support of private businesses, the U.S. Congress, and federal agencies might be sought as well. If the compact can be successfully formed—itself a major element in proof of concept—the foundations and other early contributors will have contributed to a fundamental, long-term change in the role of research and development in the delivery of education in the United States. Because education is widely held to be the route to upward mobility and the foundation of American democracy, we think the vision of SERP should have broad appeal to funders. And in contributing to a SERP launch, they will have supported the creation of an infrastructure that will facilitate their contribution to effective educational reform in the future.

While garnering commitments will be the most immediate task, there are several others that will be required for successful launch of the Strategic Education Research Partnership:

1. *Recruiting Key Leaders.* Identifying a first-rate executive director, the research and development department director, and the co-directors for at least the first research network will be critical to sending a strong signal regarding the quality of the SERP effort.
2. *Establishing Relationships with a Small Set of Field Sites.* As suggested in Chapter 4, we expect early field sites to consist of schools, districts, and schools of education that are already comfortable with, and interested in, partnering for purposes of research. But even with the most interested and experienced partners, the terms and arrangements for participation must be carefully negotiated during the start-up period.
3. *Inaugural Programs.* Once the leadership of SERP is recruited, initial research and development program commitments will need to be made. A report of the separate SERP Panel on Learning and Instruction provides an illustrative agenda for one network. Our committee also commissioned a very preliminary synthesis of the research literature on organizational change and the transfer of knowledge in organizations[2] as a modest first step in the development of a research agenda for a schools-as-organizations research network. These two illustrative research agendas provide potential seed corn for the inaugural SERP research programs.

   Launching a venture of this sort requires the imagination to see possibilities that lie beyond the horizon, a realistic vision of what can be done now, and a sensible plan to get from here to there. Those who fund the launch phase must recognize that one of the first tasks is to frame the inaugural agenda in ways that

---

[2]Available from the National Research Council, Committee on a Strategic Education Research Partnership, upon request.

will enable high-quality and productive work at a level of effort that matches the early resources, and then to use that to build up to the ambitious program recommended here and in the planning documents. Choosing particular early commitments will require an immediate effort to negotiate priorities among the new leadership, the first board of governors, and a newly formed advisory board. Having broad buy-in at the outset will be important to the ultimate success of SERP. We think the time spent in deliberation among these groups during the first two years of start-up will be well worth the investment.

4. *Legal and Organizational Specifications.* As the particulars of the SERP organization are worked out among the major founding partners, legal and organizational specifications will need to be drawn up. As the SERP coalition comes together, the partners will make final decisions about governance and organizational structure. The first-round decisions concern the nature of the new venture. But second-level issues also need to be addressed. Would SERP benefit by being housed early on in an existing host institution so as to take advantage of established grant-making, personnel, and other support functions? If so, which institutions are viable candidates?

Other legal questions would need to be answered as well. How would SERP deal with intellectual property rights and patents? These questions must be thought through carefully if SERP is to maintain the perception of a world-class institution and avoid financial conflicts of interest.

5. *Attracting Other Partners.* The SERP initiative is seeking to generate new sources of support and to bring new players to the table. The degree of interest in improving education gives us confidence that the private sector can be engaged much more heavily than heretofore in supporting a focused program of applications-oriented education research. In addition to attracting new philanthropic partners from business, SERP will work with business leaders to see if there are productive ways to involve private investment capital.

6. *Wide and Deep Consultation.* A central tenet of the SERP initiative is that fruitful collaborations among the research, practice, and policy communities are the required building blocks for making schools, classrooms, and teachers receptive to research and research useful to them. The launch team will need to give these communities a strong voice in shaping the enterprise. Major consultations will therefore be needed to collect the concerns and suggestions of the interested parties, to allow for adjustments in SERP design and process as useful suggestions are received, and to build the active public and private support needed to launch and operate a successful Strategic Education Research Partnership.

· ·

TAKING OFF

This committee, and the committee that preceded it, brought a great deal of skepticism to the table: skepticism about the ability to focus researchers on work that is relevant to practice, about getting practitioners to use research knowledge, and about the ability to create change in so complex, and behavior dependent, a system. We were confronted with a sobering history of failed efforts to improve education research and development, with an education research base with a weak reputation for quality, and by examples of some high-quality research and development that has failed to significantly penetrate the education system.

Yet this committee, like the committee that preceded it, concludes its work with optimism. Failures of the past and disappointments of the present, we believe, have identifiable contributors. It is possible to take a different approach. The SERP proposal is indeed different: different in its emphasis on use-inspired research carried out in school settings, different in the partnership between research and practice that infuses every aspect of the proposed effort, and different in the coherence of research and development program it envisions.

Program coherence means that research and product development would be joined, so that tested ideas are incorporated into teaching tools, and effective teaching practices and programs support new hypotheses about learning and instruction that can be incorporated into the shared knowledge base. The emphasis on program coherence would also be seen in the integration of research and development on learning, instruction, assessment, teacher education, school organization, and education policy so that new knowledge can be channeled into improved outcomes. Finally, program coherence would mean that promising research and development would be carried through stages of evaluation, replication in a range of school environments, and taking innovations to scale in iterative processes that spur continual improvement.

Doing such linked work will require the mobilization of many talents and resources. It will take sustained commitment for a decade to start it well, and continued, steady commitment to build a mature research and development capacity for education. A *sustained* effort to build a *coherent* research and development infrastructure in education has not failed in the past. It has simply never been tried.

With this report SERP ends as a National Academies activity and begins a new chapter. Conceived and nurtured as an initiative of the National Academies, its future success now must hinge on the will and resources of a broad coalition of partners committed to improving student learning in the United States. The National Academies recognize the critical importance of improving education in this nation and therefore stand ready to support the partners in SERP as they move forward to shape the SERP agenda and implement the bold ideas set forth in this report.

References

Anderson, J.
    1983   *The Architecture of Cognition.* Cambridge, MA: Harvard University Press.

Anderson, J.R., A.T. Corbett, K.R. Koedinger, and R. Pelletier
    1995   Cognitive tutors: Lessons learned. *Journal of the Learning Sciences* 4(2):167-207.

Beck, I.L., M.G. McKeown, R.L. Hamilton, and L. Kucan
    1997   *Questioning the Author: An Approach for Enhancing Student Engagement with Text.* Newark, DE: International Reading Association.

Briars, D.J., and L.B. Resnick
    2000   Standards, assessment—and what else? The essential elements of standards-based school improvement. Los Angeles: Center for the Study of Evaluation, UCLA (http://www.cse.ucla.edu/CRESST/Reports/TECH528.pdf).

Carpenter, T.P., E.T. Fennema, and M.L Frank
    1996   Cognitively guided instruction: A knowledge base for reform in primary mathematics instruction. *The Elementary School Journal* 97:3-20.

Case, R., and R. Sandieson
    1987   *General Development Constraints on the Acquisition of Special Procedures (and Vice Versa).* Paper presented at the annual meeting of the American Educational Research Association, Baltimore, April.

Case, R., S. Griffin, and W.M. Kelly
    1999   Socioeconomic gradients in mathematical ability and their responsiveness to intervention during early childhood. Pp. 125-149 in *Developmental Health and the Wealth of Nations: Social, Biolgical, and Educational Dynamics.* D.P. Keating and C. Hertzman, eds. New York: The Guilford Press.

Chinn, C.A., and R.C. Anderson
    1998   The structure of discussions that promote reasoning. *Teacher's College Record* 100: 51315-51368.

Consortium on Chicago School Research
    2003   Brief History of Chicago School Reform. Available on line at http://www.consortium-chicago.org/aboutus/ui002.html. Accessed February 21, 2003.

DiSessa, A.
    1982   Unlearning Aristotelian physics: A study of knowledge-base learning *Cognitive Science* 6:37–75.

Education Development Center, Inc.
 2001   *Curriculum Summaries.* Newton, MA: K-12 Mathematics Curriculum Center.

Elliott, E.
 2002   *Three Visions for Investment in Education Research: An insider's recollections from four decades in Federal policy and practice* (January, 2002). Paper prepared for the SERP Committee, National Research Council, Washington, DC.

Fallon, D.
 2001   *The Amazing Miss A and Why We Should Care About Her.* University of South Carolina, College of Education.

Ferguson, R.
 1991   Paying for public education: New evidence on how and why money matters. *Harvard Journal on Legislation* 28(Summer):465-498.

Ferguson, R.F., and H.F. Ladd
 1996   How and Why Money Matters: An Analysis of Alabama Schools. Pp. 265-298 in *Holding Schools Accountable.* H. Ladd, ed. Washington, DC: Brookings Institution.

Fuson, K.C, W.M. Carroll, and J.V. Drueck
 2000   Achievement results for second and third graders using the standards-based curriculum everyday mathematics. *Journal for Research in Mathematics Education* 31(3):277-295.

Gardner, J.
 1964   *Report of the President's Task Force on Education.* (November 14, 1964). The report is available at the LBJ Presidential Library, Austin, TX.

Griffin, S., and R. Case
 1997   Re-thinking the primary school math curriculum: An approach based on cognitive science. *Issues in Education* 3(1):1-49.

Mannes, S.M., and W. Kintsch
 1987   Knowledge organization and text organization. *Cognition and Instruction* 4:91-115.

National Council of Teachers of Mathematics
 1989   *Curriculum and Evaluation Standards for School Mathematics.* Reston, VA.
 2000   *Principles and Standards for School Mathematics.* Reston, VA.

National Institute of Child Health and Human Development
 2000   Report of the National Reading Panel. Teaching children to read: An evidence-based assessment of the scientific research literature on reading and its implications for reading instructions. (NIH Publication No. 00-4769). Washington, DC: U.S. Government Printing Office.

National Research Council
 1992   *Research and Education Reform: Roles for the Office of Educational Research and Improvement.* R.C. Atkinson and G.B. Jackson, eds. Committee on the Federal Role in Education Research. Washington, DC: National Academy Press.
 1998   *Preventing Reading Difficulties in Young Children.* C.E. Snow, M. Burns, and R. Griffin, eds. Washington, DC: National Academy Press.
 1999   *Improving Student Learning: A Strategic Plan for Education Research and Its Utilization.* Commission on Behavioral and Social Sciences and Education. Washington, DC: National Academy Press.

2000 *How People Learn: Brain, Mind, Experience, and School.* J.D. Bransford, A.L. Brown, and R.R. Cocking, eds. Commission on Behavioral and Social Sciences and Education. Washington, DC: National Academy Press.

2001 *Knowing What Students Know: The Science and Design of Educational Assessment.* J.W. Pellegrino, N. Chudowsky, and R. Glaser, eds. Washington, DC: National Academy Press.

2002a *Attracting PhDs to K-12 Education: A Demonstration Program for Science, Mathematics, and Technology.* Division of Behavioral and Social Sciences and Education and Division of Policy and Global Affairs. Washington, DC: National Academy Press.

2002b *Scientific Research in Education.* R. Shavelson and L. Towne, eds. Washington, DC: National Academy Press.

2003a Teaching mathematics in the primary grades: fostering the development of whole number sense. Sharon Griffin, author. In *How Students Learn.* Washington, DC: The National Academies Press.

2003b *Learning and Instruction: A SERP Research Agenda.* M.S. Donovan and J.W. Pellegrino, eds. Washington, DC: The National Academies Press.

Palincsar, A.S.
1986 The role of dialogue in providing scaffolded instruction. *Educational Psychologist* 21(1&2): 73-98.

Palincsar, A.S., and A.L. Brown
1984 Reciprocal teaching of comprehension-fostering and comprehension-monitoring activities. *Cognition and Instruction* 1:117-175.

Palincsar, A.S., and L.R. Herrenkohl
2002 Designing collaborative learning contexts. *Theory Into Practice* 41(1): 26-32.

Palincsar, A.S., D.D. Stevens, and J.R. Gavelek
1989 Collaborating with teachers in the interest of student collaboration. *International Journal of Educational Research*, 13:41-53.

Polanyi, M.
1967 *The Tacit Dimension.* Garden City, NJ: Doubleday Anchor.

Pressley, M., C.J. Johnson, S. Symons, J.A. McGoldrick, and J.A. Kurita
1989 Strategies that improve children's memory and comprehension of text. *Elementary School Journal* 90(1):3-32.

Public Papers of the President
1970 Special Message to the Congress on Education Reform, March 3, 1970. Available from the Office of the Federal Register, National Archives and Records Administration, Washington, DC.

RAND
2002a Reading for Understanding: Toward an R&D Program in Reading Comprehension. RAND Reading Study Group. C. Snow, Chair. Prepared for the Office of Education Research and Improvement (OERI).

2002b *Mathematical Proficiency for All Students: Toward a Strategic Research and Development Program in Mathematics Education.* RAND Mathematics Study Panel. Deborah Loewenberg Ball, Chair. DRU-2773-OERI.

Roderick, M., A.S. Bryk, B.A. Jacob, J.Q. Easton, and E. Allensworth.
1998 *Ending Social Promotion: Results from the First Two Years.* Chicago: Consortium on Chicago School Research.

Roderick, M., J. Nagaoka, J. Bacon, and J.Q. Easton
1999 *Update: Ending Social Promotion.* Chicago: Consortium on Chicago School Research.

Schifter, D., V. Bastable, and S.J. Russell
2000   *Developing Mathematical Ideas.* Newton, MA: Education Development Center

Schneps, M., and P. Sadler
1987   *A Private Universe.* Video. Cambridge, MA; Washington, DC: Annenberg/CPB: Pyramid Film and Video.

Schofield, J.W., D. Evans-Rhodes, and B.R. Huber
1990   Artificial intelligence in the classroom: The impact of a computer-based tutor on teachers and students. *Social Science Computer Review* 8(1):24-41.

Strauss, R.P., and E.A. Sawyer
1986   Some new evidence on teacher and student competencies. *Economics of Education Review* 5(1):41-48.

Tivnan, T.
2002   Final Report to the U.S. Department of Education, Planning and Evaluation Service, Assessing Literacy Models in the Boston Public Schools. Unpublished report, Harvard Graduate School of Education.

The University of Chicago School Mathematics Project
1995   *Everyday Mathematics: Teacher's Manual and Lesson Guide.* Evanston, IL: Everyday Learning Corporation.

U.S. Department of Education, National Center for Education Statistics
2001a *Digest of Education Statistics.* Washington, DC: U.S. Government Printing Office.
2001b *Federal Support for Education: Fiscal Years 1980 to 2001,* NCES 2002-129. Written by C M. Hoffman. Washington, DC: U.S. Government Printing Office.

Voshiadou, S., and W.F. Brewer
1989   The Concept of the Earth's Shape: A Study of Conceptual Change in Childhood. Unpublished paper. Center for the Study of Reading, University of Illinois, Champaign.

White, B.Y., and J.R. Frederiksen
1998   Inquiry, modeling, and metacognition: Making science accessible to all students. *Cognition and Instruction* 16(1):3-118.

Wood, T. and P. Sellers
1997   Deepening the analysis: Longitudinal assessment of a problem-centered mathematics program. *Journal for Research in Mathematics Education* 28(2):163-186.

A Federal Investments in Education Research: A Sobering History

The federal government has been by far the largest supporter of education research in this country, and so the history of its investments is an important backdrop to thinking about SERP. The record of the government's continuing efforts over four decades to develop a significant role for research in the U.S. Department of Education and its predecessor agencies was summarized for the committee by Emerson Elliott (2002).

The current leadership of the U.S. Department of Education and its Institute for Education Sciences (IES) has a strong presidential mandate to strengthen the agency's capacity to bring science to the service of education reform. This has also been true on two prior occasions: with the inauguration of President Lyndon B. Johnson's Great Society program and then again during the Nixon administration.

In 1964 Johnson established a President's Task Force on Education, chaired by John Gardner, then president of the Carnegie Corporation and later to become secretary of the U.S. Department of Health, Education, and Welfare. This group produced the first formal and public vision for what research in education might accomplish and how that might be made to happen. The vision and the rhetoric with which it is expressed are in some regards remarkably similar to our own (Gardner, 1964):

> When viewed against the $33 billion we spend annually on education at all levels, the support for research, even as augmented by foundations and private corporations, is a trickle. This has to be changed. We now know beyond all doubt that, educationally speaking, the old ways of doing things will not solve our

problems . . . . A massive burst of innovation is called for. . . . We need a system designed for continuous renewal, a system in which reappraisal and innovation are built in . . . . [A]bove all, what is taught and how it is taught must change.

Like the SERP initiative, the 1964 task force was primarily interested in making research useful to practice (Gardner, 1964):

The problem today is not only one of innovation, but of converting new ideas into forms useable in the classroom, testing their applicability in the field, disseminating the proven ideas throughout the educational system.

The Gardner report envisioned close (although, unlike SERP, not collaborative) links between research and practice (Gardner, 1964):

The laboratories would have to be intimately related to the educational system at all levels. They would have close ties with the State departments of education. They would establish links with numerous schools (or school systems) for the sake of teacher training and the field testing of new programs. It would also be essential that each laboratory have some kind of affiliation with a neighboring university.

The major "innovation" proposed in the Gardner report was federal aid for the establishment of large-scale national education laboratories, which would develop and disseminate ideas and programs for improving educational practices throughout the country (Gardner, 1964):

There should be at least a dozen major laboratories and perhaps two or three dozen more that are specialized or less ambitious in scope. By "laboratories" we do not mean small-scale efforts, operating out of a corner of a department of education, rooted in the interests of a few faculty members, and having little connection with the daily practice of education in the community. As we conceive them, the laboratories would be more closely akin to the great national laboratories of the Atomic Energy Commission and should share many of their features. Improvement or innovation in the education of our children is at least as important as the maintenance of our defense and deserves a similar effort.

The whole package was estimated to reach a cost of $250 million (in 1964 dollars) annually after five years.

"Unfortunately," writes Elliott (2002), "we never learned what national educational laboratories might achieve because they were never created." The career staff at the Office of Education (OE) neither read the Gardner report nor gave its recommendation for national laboratories serious consideration. The statutory prohibition on OE influence over the curriculum and management of schools occasioned deep concern about political fallout from anything in education with the word "national" attached to it. Moreover, the OE appropriations that could realistically be anticipated for research were clearly not sufficient to the Gardner vision, even in the heady days of the Great Society education legislation of 1965.

Instead, regional educational laboratories were created and are still with us. They are, in Elliott's judgment, "a set of small institutions with ill-defined missions," for which federal policy "has been reformulated by almost every head of education research since 1965—or perhaps a more accurate phrase, the heads of research have tried to reformulate Federal policy."

The second great vision for research came from the pen of Daniel Patrick Moynihan early in President Nixon's administration (Public Papers of the President, 1970). The key feature of this reform proposal from the president to Congress was the creation of an education research agency, independent from the Office of Education of the Department of Health, Education, and Welfare, that would be known as the National Institute of Education (NIE).

The idea was for NIE to link educational research and experimentation across federal agencies to "the attainment of particular national educational goals." The president's message made clear that the institute would devise its own agenda—setting priorities, taking the lead in measurement of education output, developing a coherent approach, serving as an objective national body, and evaluating new departures in teaching.

In contrast to the Gardner report, the Moynihan document made no mention of "development." But it shared with Gardner a view about who should conduct research—scholars from different disciplines, largely through universities, nonprofits, and other organizations—as well as a budget projection of $250 million annually (more than $1 billion in today's dollars).

What happened? NIE was created two years later with, as Elliott puts it, a notable lack of enthusiasm, especially on the Senate side. Its operations began not with the singleness of purpose evinced in the president's message to Congress, but instead with the transfer of existing research programs from the

Office of Education. Before NIE had established and staffed its own agenda, it had to take on direct management responsibilities for ongoing programs, and it never really recovered the initiative. In addition, political tensions between Congress and the administration—in particular, the voucher program, a top administration priority—had a rapid and ultimately crippling effect. In a dramatic signal of what was to come, the institute received an appropriation mark of zero from the Senate in 1974. Funding for NIE plummeted and continued to spiral downward when its functions were assumed by the Office of Educational Research and Development. Between 1973 and 1989, the total decline (in constant 1990 dollars) was 88 percent (National Research Council, 1992:95).

For all its problems, NIE did have enormous success in attracting talented people who went on to make important contributions to the advancement of education and social policy. NIE also planned and began lines of research that have made a continuing contribution to education, such as on capacity building/effective schools; reading; teaching; the first Title I evaluation; and the National Education Library, which NIE literally resurrected from warehouse storage.

But it did not become the independent and strategic research agency envisioned. Reflecting on the period, Elliott writes that "those of us who were a part of those early years of NIE learned how personal views of the public, the Congress, and the Administration cannot be separated from an education research agenda in the U.S. Department of Education. The committee also learned that the Department of Education probably differs from other agencies through which the federal government invests in education research (e.g., the National Science Foundation, the National Institute for Child Health and Human Development, the Office of Naval Research, and the Defense Advanced Research Projects Agency) *in which the perspectives and actions of researchers appear to be a steadier guide to progress*" (emphasis added).

Summing up his 40-plus years as a participant in this history, Elliott writes (2002): "We have a Department of Education research effort that is the merest shadow of either the Gardner or the Moynihan/Nixon visions. . . ." With at least 14 assistant secretaries and heads of research (and many acting assistant secretaries and directors) in the past 30 years, it has been difficult to sustain an investment in serious research and build momentum. Elliott finds, instead, a "four-decade long record of *lack* of continuity, or synthesis, or efforts to accumulate what has been learned from research and from practice; lack of strong research methodologies and of effectively implemented focus or priorities." He concludes also that "hot-button issues—such as vouchers or curriculum development—are nearly impossible to investigate through the Department of Education because the motives of any who propose such work are suspect."

From this first-person account we take many lessons, not all of them cautionary. The success that NIE had in attracting first-rate talent to the cause of improving education with a strong vision and plan of action lends credibility to our aspirations for the SERP endeavor. Public concern about and belief in education is there throughout. Moreover, to know that the best and brightest in earlier generations saw the great potential for research to contribute to education practice is important, even if we have not yet realized that potential.

One of our key judgments that we see confirmed in this history is that the needs and rhythms of politics and research are fundamentally different. Although the two cannot and should not be entirely divorced, distance is important. The accumulation of knowledge that is needed to fuel change and innovation in complex systems requires coherence and continuity and staying power.

Equally important, of course, is the matter of funding. Research is a cumulative process; advances in knowledge come incrementally and by building on what has gone before. No matter how good the plan or how talented the people, without long-term, stable funding, a powerful accumulation of research is simply not possible. The history of NIE shows how quickly the funding can disappear. Impact is also a function of level of effort (i.e., sufficiency of funding). As a 1994 National Research Council report on the Office of Education Research and Improvement described in some detail, the funding available for education research and development has lagged far behind federal funding for research in agriculture, health, defense, and transportation, based on whatever measure one might choose (National Research Council, 1992:95-106).

REFERENCES

Elliott, E.

    2002   *Three Visions for Investment in Education Research: An Insider's Recollections from Four Decades in Federal Policy and Practice* (January, 2002). Paper prepared for the SERP Committee, National Research Council, Washington, DC.

Gardner, J.

    1964   *Report of the President's Task Force on Education.* (November 14, 1964). The report is available at the LBJ Presidential Library, Austin, TX.

National Research Council

    1992   *Research and Education Reform: Roles for the Office of Educational Research and Improvement.* Committee on the Federal Role in Education Research. R.C. Atkinson and G.B. Jackson, eds. Washington, DC: National Academy Press.

Public Papers of the President

    1970   Special Message to the Congress on Education Reform, March 3, 1970. Available from the Office of the Federal Register, National Archives and Records Administration, Washington, DC.

B
SERP Cost Projections: A Scenario for the Proof-of-Concept Period

n order to facilitate discussion, the committee believes it is important to provide very rough, ball-park figures for the cost of a SERP start-up. The problem, of course, is that the pace of start-up—the number of initial research and development initiatives, the number of initial field sites, and the growth rate for each organizational activity—will be determined by the available resources, the rate at which quality personnel can be recruited, and by critical decisions made by the early management team. This, then, should be viewed as no more than a single scenario for cost projections under a set of assumptions that may differ in any number of respects from those that characterize an actual SERP launch. The assumptions are clearly specified so that a reader can judge the general impact of alternative assumptions.

The cost estimates were developed by a consultant under parameters provided by the committee with regard to costs for personnel with the expertise and training required for the SERP program, and for data collection and other aspects of research. Rates for fringe benefits, overhead, and general and administrative costs (G&A) were assumed for purposes of estimation, but the actual costs in this category will depend on the institutional setting in which the SERP enterprise is launched.

Not included in these estimates is the cost of an initial two-year "launch" period, during which an effort to build support for the enterprise and to recruit key personnel would be undertaken. Year one costs, then, are estimates for the first year of a functioning research and development enterprise, but the third year into SERP launch (see Table B.1).

PRICING AND FREQUENCY ASSUMPTIONS

Years 1-7

Core Staffing

Load factors

> Fringe benefits: 26% of salaries
> Overhead: 30% of salaries & fringes
> General & administrative: 19% of all costs

For example: The full load on a $100,000 salary would be computed as follows:

> [($100,000 * 0.26) * 1.30] * 1.19 =
> ($126,000 * 1.63) * 1.19 =
> $163,800 * 1.19 = $194,922

Therefore, the full load factor is 1.949 ($194,922/$100,000)

Base Salaries—Senior Professional Staff—Core

Assumption A: Director's salary is set at $300,000 in Year 1, plus 2 senior administrative persons at $60,000 each.

Assumption B: 2 deputies' salaries are set at $150,000 each in Year 1, plus 1 senior administrative person per deputy at $60,000 each.

Assumption C: Senior planning officer, senior communications officer, and senior development officer salaries are set at $150,000 each in Year 1, plus 1 senior administrative person per officer at $60,000 each

Assumption D: 12 senior program officers (expert researchers and practitioners) and 2 web site design specialists salaries are set at $128,700 in Year 1, plus 1 administrative support person per program officer and design specialist at $50,000 each for 8 positions and $40,000 each for the other 6 positions.

Assumption E: 2 professional staff—a financial officer and a grants manager. The financial officer is needed for the full term of Year 1; the grants manager will come on halfway through Year 1. Salaries for both positions are set at $100,000 in Year 1, plus 1 administrative support person for each of the positions at $30,000 each.

The full-load factor of 1.949 is applied to these base salaries to project costs of each fully loaded core staff person (director, deputies, senior planning officer, senior communications officer, senior development officer, senior program officers, design specialists, finance officer, and grants manager). For example, the fully loaded costs for each of the following positions for Year 1 would be:

Director's base salary:	$300,000
2 senior administrative persons' base salary:	120,000
Total base salaries:	420,000
Applying full load factor (1.949 * total base)	$818,580
Deputy's base salary	$150,000
1 senior administrative person's salary	60,000
Total base salaries:	210,000
Applying full load factor (1.949 * total base)	$409,290
Planning officer's base salary	$150,000
1 senior administrative person's salary	60,000
Total base salaries:	210,000
Applying full load factor (1.949 * total base)	$409,290
Senior program officer's base salary:	$128,700
Administrative support person base salary[1]:	45,715
Total base salaries:	173,700
Applying full load factor (1.949 * total base)	$338,541
Finance officer's base salary:	$100,000
1 administrative support person's salary:	30,000
Total base salaries:	130,000
Applying full load factor (1.949 * total base)	$253,370

Staffing Numbers

In the years subsequent to Year 1, there will be the following additions to the core staff:

As each network comes on line (e.g., learning and instruction in Year 2 and schools as organizations in Year 3), 2 fully loaded core program staff are added.

For each additional 3 projects in a Network, an additional 2 fully loaded core program staff also are added.

In Year 3, there are added 1 additional administrative support person to each of the financial officer and grants manager positions (i.e., 2 administrative support persons for each in Year 3). In Year 4, there is added another additional administrative support person to the grants manager position (for a total of 3 administrative support persons for the grants manager in Year 4). In Year 5, there is added another additional adminis-

---

[1] $45,715 is the mean, i.e., 8 @ $50,000 and 6 @ $40,000.

trative support person to the financial officer position (for a total of 3 administrative support persons for both the grants manager and financial officer in Year 5 and subsequent years).

Annual Salary Increases

A 5% factor has been used to increase base salaries in Year 2, and a 5% factor to increase base salaries from Year 2 to Year 3, and the same 5% factor for subsequent years.

Honoraria for Advisory Board Members

No honoraria are included for members of the governing board. For the members of the advisory boards, an honorarium of $500 per day is assumed; a total of $120,000 in Year 1. A 5% factor has been used to increase honoraria in Year 2 and in subsequent years through Year 7.

Network Staffing

Start Year

Year 2 is the start year. There is no network staffing projected for Year 1.

Load Factors

The load factors applied to network staff positions (researchers, master teachers, senior fellows, junior fellows) are as follows:

Fringe benefits:	26% of salaries
Offsite overhead:	30% of salaries & fringes
General & administration:	19% of all costs

Resulting is a load factor of 1.949
The load factors applied to field site teachers are:

Fringe benefits:	26% of salaries
Pass through:	3%
General & administration:	19% of all costs

The resulting load factor is 1.54.

Base Salaries

The following base salaries for Year 2 are used:

Researcher:	$125,000
Master teacher:	100,000
Senior fellow:	100,000
Junior fellow:	75,000
Field site teachers:	42,000 (60% of $70,000)

Annual Salary Increases

A 5% factor has been used to increase base salaries in Year 3, and a 5% factor to increase base salaries from Year 3 to Year 4, and the same 5% factor for Year 5.

Teacher Training Stipends

Teacher training stipends for teachers receiving training and/or involved in training are set at $125 per day with no load. For example, in Year 2 the assumption is that summer training courses for teachers will involve 25 teachers for 15 days at $125 per day. Thus, the full stipend cost for this example would be:

($125 * 15 days) * 25 teachers =
$1,875 * 25 = $46,875

The 5% inflation factor also has been applied to the stipends.

Travel

Professional Staff—Core and Network

Four types of travel trips are used: (1) three-day trip, (2) two-day trip, (3) one-day trip, and (4) three-day weekend trip. In the latter case, the costs of the three-day weekend trip are estimated to be appreciably lower than the regular three-day trip (1) because of a reduction in rates for "stay-over Saturday night" airfares and, to a lesser extent, reductions in hotel/motel rates. The costs included are air and/or ground travel, lodging, and meals. The estimated costs of each type of trip are as follows:

Three-day trip:	$1,250
Two-day trip:	1,100
One-day trip:	850
Three-day weekend trip:	900

Teachers Professional Development

The majority of travel costs for professional development will be limited to mileage reimbursement for one-way travel in excess of 10 miles; reimbursement will be at the federal rate of 34.5 cents/mile. In instances in which one-way travel exceeds 50 miles, the estimates identified above are used.

Governing Board and Advisory Boards

The Professional Staff—Core and Network cost assumptions for travel have been used for travel of members of the governing board and advisory boards, namely:

Four types of travel trips are used: (1) three-day trip, (2) two-day trip, (3) one-day trip, and (4) three-day weekend trip. In the latter case, the costs of the three-day weekend trip are estimated to be appreciably lower than the regular three-day trip (1) because of a reduction in rates for "stay-over Saturday night" airfares and, to a lesser extent, reductions in hotel/motel rates. The costs included are air and/or ground travel, lodging, and meals. The estimated costs of each type of trip are as follows:

Three-day trip:	$1,250
Two-day trip:	1,100
One-day trip:	850
Three-day weekend trip:	900

The assumptions are that the governing board will be comprised of 20 members, will meet three times a year, the meetings will be a full two days each during the week and thus require three-day trips. In addition, there may be need for one one-day meeting and thus require one additional two-day trip.

The assumptions are that each of the advisory boards will be comprised of 10 members, will meet three times a year, and the meetings will be one day during the week and thus require two-day trips. In addition, each advisory board may have need for an additional three one-day meetings and thus require an additional three two-day trips.

Annual Inflation Factor

A 5% annual inflation factor has been applied to travel costs from Year 1 to Year 2, and so on through Year 7.

Database Systems

The amount of $10 million is included in core operations in Year 1 to address the technical, logistical, and legal issues of setting up databases in participating states/school systems to be used by networks for their research. This amount has been increased annually by a 5% inflation factor.

Web-Based Communications

The amount of $250,000 has been included in core operations in Year 1 to support the development of a web-based communication system. This amount has been increased annually by a factor of 1.25 through Year 7.

Contracts—Network Operations

It is likely that there may be need for contracted services for competitively bid research and development contractors, technical assistance groups, technology contractors, and additional studies.

Consequently, and quite arbitrarily, the fixed amount of $300,000 has been included in Year 2, and through Year 7 with a 5% annual inflator, for each research project under way in each of the networks operating in those years.

In addition, $14,000/year for office rental space has been included for each of the field-based projects. The initial office rental space figure for a specific network field-based project is set at the year the project comes online at $14,000, adjusted for 5% annual inflation from Year 1.

Consultants

There may be need for professional and consultant services by persons who are members of a particular profession or who possess a special skill, including regularly engaged classroom teachers and other local district and school practitioners (as separate from teachers receiving training and/or otherwise involved in training sessions; these would receive stipends in keeping with the assumptions set forth in network staffing under Teacher Professional Development Stipends).

Consequently, the fixed amount of $50,000 has been included in Year 2, and through Year 7 with a 5% annual inflator, for each research project under way in each of the networks operating in those years.

Other Related Costs

All other related costs—including legal and auditing, equipment, postage, publications/printing, and the like—are assumed to be covered by the 30% overhead and 19% general and administrative loads.

NETWORK PROGRAM ASSUMPTIONS

Years 1-7

Individual Project Costs

There are two separate fixed amounts, adjusted annually for 5% inflation, for the costs of each of 10 projects. One cost is for a regular project. The other cost is for a field-based project.

The amount, unadjusted in Year 2 (the start year for network activity), for a regular project is $7,073,571 and is shown in Table B.2. The amount, unadjusted in Year 2 (the Start Year for Network activity), for a field-based project is $9,593,571. This number reflects the costs shown in Table B-2 plus additional costs, shown in Table B.3. In summary:

Total for regular:	$7,073,571
Total for the field-based add-on:	$2,520,000
Total Cost for Field-Based:	**$9,593,571**

One assumption underlying the projected amounts of $7,073,571 and $9,593,571 is that each project, whether regular or field-based, will require the same or similar staffing and travel as do the initial regular and field-based projects in the Learning and Instruction Network in Year 2 (the start year for the networks). The $7,073,571 and $9,593,571 numbers are judgment-based estimates; still, they would appear to be reasonable beginnings for projecting costs of the network projects, both regular and field-based. These amounts in reality, of course, will vary considerably—some higher, some lower.

Phasing of Networks and Network Projects

The assumption for the seven-year proof-of-concept period is that two networks will be operating. By Year 7, the first and second networks will have 10 projects under way—5 field-based and 5 regular. The first network in operation is Learning and Instruction. The second network is schools as organizations.

Table B.1 presents the year each network (2) and each network project is phased in. The field-based projects are identified with an asterisk. For example, Project 1 in the Learning and Instruction Network, a field-based project, begins in Year 2 and runs through Year 7. Project 3 in the schools as organizations network, a field-based project, begins in Year 6 and runs through Year 7, and so on. Just as the fixed amount, adjusted annually for 5% inflation, for the costs of each of the network projects is for illustrative purposes, so is the phasing-in scheme used for networks and network projects.

TABLE B.1 Summary Cost Projections
7 Years and 2 Networks

Category	Year 1	Year 2	Year 3	Year 4	Year 5	Year 6	Year 7
Core Organization							
Management Staff—full load	$2,865,030	$3,131,069	$3,287,622	$3,452,003	$3,624,603	$3,805,833	$3,996,125
Research Staff—full load	$4,720,088	$4,874,235	$5,950,381	$6,247,900	$7,383,293	$8,616,606	$12,676,858
Administration Staff—full load	$380,005	$532,077	$687,607	$789,674	$900,228	$945,240	$992,502
Staff Travel	$231,350	$242,918	$255,063	$267,817	$281,207	$295,268	$310,031
Database Development	$10,000,000	$10,500,000	$11,025,000	$11,576,250	$12,155,063	$12,762,816	$13,400,956
Web-based Communication	$250,000	$312,500	$390,625	$488,281	$610,352	$762,939	$953,674
Governing Board							
Travel	$92,000	$96,600	$101,430	$106,502	$111,827	$117,418	$123,289
Advisory Boards							
Honoraria	$120,000	$126,000	$132,300	$138,915	$145,861	$153,154	$160,811
Travel	$132,000	$138,600	$145,530	$152,807	$160,447	$168,469	$176,893
Networks							
Learning & Instruction							
Project 1*		$9,593,571	$10,073,250	$10,576,912	$11,105,758	$11,661,046	$12,244,098
Project 2			$7,427,250	$7,798,613	$8,188,543	$8,597,970	$9,027,869
Project 3*				$10,576,912	$11,105,758	$11,661,045	$12,244,098
Project 4					$7,798,612	$8,188,543	$8,597,970
Project 5*						$11,661,045	$12,244,097
Project 6							$8,597,970
Schools as Organizations							
Project 1*			$10,073,250	$10,576,913	$11,105,758	$11,661,046	$12,244,098
Project 2				$7,798,613	$8,188,544	$8,597,971	$9,027,869
Project 3*						$11,661,046	$12,244,098
Project 4							$9,027,869
TOTALS:	$18,790,473	$29,547,570	$49,549,308	$70,548,110	$82,865,852	$111,317,454	$138,291,176

7 Yr Total: $500,909,942

$501 million

TABLE B.2 Individual Project Costs
L & I Network

Position	Base	Number	Load factor	Fully loaded cost	
Regular					
Researchers	$125,000	8	1.949	$1,949,000	
Admin support	$45,000	4	1.949	$701,640	
Master teachers	$100,000	2	1.949	$389,800	
Admin support	$45,000	1	1.949	$87,705	
Senior fellows	$100,000	8	1.949	$1,559,200	
Junior fellows	$75,000	8	1.949	$1,169,400	
Admin support	$45,000	2	1.949	$701,640	$6,558,385
Contracts					
Basic				$300,000	$300,000
Consultants				$50,000	$50,000

Travel—Network Staff

Position	Cost	Number	Total	
Researcher				
Three-day	$1,313	8	$10,504	
Two-day	$1,155	40	$46,200	
One-day	$893	16	$14,288	
Three-day weekend	$945	8	$7,560	
				$78,552
Master teacher				
Three-day	$1,313	2	$2,626	
Two-day	$1,155	10	$11,550	
One-day	$893	4	$3,572	
Three-day weekend	$945	2	$1,890	
				$19,638
Senior fellow				
Three-day	$1,313	2	$2,626	
Two-day	$1,155	22	$25,410	
One-day	$893	4	$3,572	
Three-day weekend	$945	2	$1,890	
				$33,498
Junior fellow				
Three-day	$1,313	2	$2,626	
Two-day	$1,155	22	$25,410	
One-day	$893	4	$3,572	
Three-day weekend	$945	2	$1,890	
Field site leaders				
Two-day	$1,155	16	$18,480	
				$51,978
Total				$7,073,571

TABLE B.3 Additional Costs for a Field-Based Project

Add-on for field-based					
Field site administrator	$125,000	1	1.949	$243,625	
Admin support	$50,000	1	1.949	$97,450	
Teacher coordinator	$60,000	0.5	1.949	$58,470	
Field site teachers	$42,000	30	1.54	$1,940,400	
Stipends for teachers in summer training	$1,875	25	0	$46,875	
					$2,386,820
Travel					
Field-site leaders					
Two-day	$1,155	16		$18,480	
					$18,480
<u>Contracts</u>					
Field-based data systems				$100,000	
Space rental—field-based				$14,700	
					$114,700
Total add-on					$2,520,000

C Biographical Sketches of Committee Members and Staff

Joe B. Wyatt (*Chair*), chancellor and CEO of Vanderbilt University from 1982 to 2000, is a computer scientist who has focused on technology-based innovation in business, research, and education for 45 years. A patentee in computer-aided design systems, he has led the development and implementation of computer-based teaching models in a number of fields ranging from law to computer science. While a member of the faculty and vice president at Harvard University, he was a founding director and vice chairman of the Massachusetts Technology Development Corporation, a public venture capital company for new technology start-ups begun in 1978. Wyatt is a fellow of the American Association for the Advancement of Science, a director of several companies, a trustee of several philanthropic organizations, and a principal of the Washington Advisory Group.

John S. Reed (*Vice Chair*) retired in April 2000 as chairman and co-chief executive officer of Citigroup. Mr. Reed spent 35 years at Citicorp and played a part in the tremendous transformation that has taken place in the industry, from globalization and the advent of electronic banking, to the creation of Citigroup, a new breed of financial services firm. He also created the Citicorp Behavioral Sciences Research Council. He has served on the boards of the Russell Sage Foundation and the Center for Advanced Studies in the Behavioral and Social Sciences, the Spencer Foundation, and Massachusetts Institute of Technology. He is a fellow of the American Academy of Arts and Sciences and the American Philosophical Society.

Catherine Snow (*Vice Chair*) is the Henry Lee Shattuck professor of education at the Harvard Graduate School of Education. Her research involves language and literacy acquisition, second language acquisition, and bilingualism. She has held teaching and research positions at Erasmus University, the University of Amsterdam, the University of Cambridge, Hebrew University in Jerusalem, and Universidad Autonoma in Madrid. She was chair of the National Research Council's Committee on the Prevention of Reading Difficulties in Young Children and is currently chairing a National Academy of Education committee producing a report on educating teachers to teach reading.

Carole Ames has served as professor of educational psychology and dean of the College of Education at Michigan State University since 1993. She has also held administrative and faculty positions at the University of Illinois at Urbana-Champaign and at the University of Maryland. Her research has focused on the development of social and academic motivation in children, especially the effects of classroom structures and teaching practices on children's motivation to learn and on school and family relationships. She has published extensively on these topics, is a fellow of the American Psychological Association, and has served on the board of several professional organizations.

James N. Baron is the Walter Kenneth Kilpatrick professor of organizational behavior and human resources at Stanford University. His research interests include human resource management and organizational design, especially in emerging companies; the effects of social networks on employees; and career inequalities by gender and race. He currently serves on the advisory boards of several academic and corporate organizations.

Lloyd Bond joined the Carnegie Foundation for the Advancement of Teaching as a senior scholar in 2002, after professorships at the University of North Carolina-Greensboro (1988-2002) and the University of Pittsburgh (1976-1988). As an educational measurement specialist, he has been an associate editor and member of the editorial boards of many of the leading journals in education and psychology. A fellow of the American Psychological Association, he has served widely on scientific committees of the National Research Council, the American Psychological Association, and the American Educational Research Association. He has a Ph.D. in psychometrics from the Johns Hopkins University.

David Cohen is John Dewey collegiate professor of education and professor of public policy at the University of Michigan. His research has addressed the relations between policy and instruction, the relations between research and policy, the nature of teaching practice, efforts to reform schools and teaching, and large-scale school intervention programs. With Brian Rowan and Deborah L. Ball, he is directing the Study of Instructional Improvement, a large, longitudinal study of efforts to improve performance in high-poverty elementary schools.

Laura Cooper is the assistant superintendent for curriculum and instruction at Evanston Township High School, Evanston, Illinois. She has worked as a secondary teacher and administrator in urban and suburban districts in Arizona, Massachusetts, and Illinois and directed the Institute for Learning and Teaching at the University of Massachusetts, Boston. Her work has focused on changing classrooms and schools by valuing the craft knowledge of teachers and principals and by drawing on the research on teaching and learning. She helped create a national network of 15 school districts committed to eliminating the gap in achievement between white students and students of color, and she currently serves as the convener for the Research Practitioner Council of the Minority Student Achievement Network.

Suzanne Donovan is associate director of the National Research Council's Strategic Education Research Partnership, and study director of a project that will produce a volume for teachers entitled *How Students Learn: History, Math, and Science in the Classroom.* She was the study director for the NRC reports *Minority Students in Special and Gifted Education,* and *How People Learn: Bridging Research and Practice.* She was also a co-editor of *Eager to Learn: Educating our Preschoolers.* She has a Ph.D. in public policy from the University of California, Berkeley, and was previously on the faculty of Columbia University.

James A. Kelly, senior advisor to the SERP project, is an advisor to education organizations, government agencies, and corporations. He was the founding president of the National Board for Professional Teaching Standards, which was created in 1987 to improve teaching by offering national, voluntary, advanced professional certification to American teachers and now has certified almost 24,000 teachers as meeting the nation's first rigorous standards for accomplished teaching. He retired in October 1999. From 1970 to 1981, he served as program officer at the Ford Foundation, directing programs in education finance reform and related fields and between 1966 and 1978 was on the faculty of Columbia University, serving as assistant, associate, and adjunct professor. His career in education began as a teacher in Ladue, Missouri.

Charles Miller is chairman of Meridian Advisors, Ltd., a private, family investment partnership. Previously, he was founder and chief executive of an international investment management firm. He is chairman of the Board of Regents of the University of Texas System. In 2001, he served as a member of the education advisory committee that was appointed by President Bush to help on education issues during the administrative transition. He has served as chairman to a number of public policy committees in Texas dealing with issues ranging from education policy to business development.

Richard R. Nelson is George Blumenthal professor of international and public affairs at Columbia University. He has also taught at Yale University, Carnegie Mellon University, and Oberlin College. He has been a senior staff member of the Presidents Council of Economic Advisers and a researcher at the Rand Corporation. His central research interests have been on long-run economic change, with a particular focus on how technology advances over time and the nature and function of economic institutions. These interests led him some years ago to develop, along with Sidney Winter, *An Evolutionary Theory of Economic Change*. He has written extensively on technological advance, as well as topics in science and technology policy, and is currently interested in the evolution of human know-how, particularly in the fields of medicine and education.

Rebecca A. Palacios is a dual language program prekindergarten teacher at Lorenzo de Zavala Special Emphasis School in Corpus Christi, Texas. She was formerly the lead teacher for 3-year-olds at Texas A&M University and Corpus Christi Independent School District's Early Childhood Development Center. She is a founding director of the National Board for Professional Teaching Standards and received national board certification in 1997. Her doctoral dissertation was on the developmental appropriateness of state-adopted prekindergarten curriculum materials in Texas for prekindergarten children.

Thomas W. Payzant has served as school superintendent in Montgomery County, Pennsylvania; Eugene, Oregon; Oklahoma City; San Diego; and currently the city of Boston. In 1993, he was appointed by President Clinton to serve as assistant secretary for elementary and secondary education in the U. S. Department of Education. He worked closely with the Clinton administration to enact passage of the Goals 2000: Educate America Act and to reauthorize the Elementary and Secondary Education Act. He has written more than 30 journal articles and book reviews. In 1998, he was named one of four national finalists for Superintendent of the Year by the American Association of School Administrators.

Michael Rothschild is the William Stuart Tod professor of economics and public affairs at Princeton University. He served as dean of the Woodrow Wilson School of Public Affairs and International Affairs at Princeton University and as founding dean of the Division of Social Science at the University of California, San Diego. An economic theorist, Rothshild has developed tools for studying decision making under uncertainty and the structure of markets with asymmetric information. He has also written on education, investment, taxation, finance, and jury decision processes. He has held a Guggenheim fellowship and various research grants from the National Science Foundation and has served on the faculties of Princeton University, Harvard University, and the University of Wisconsin. He is a fellow of the American Academy of Arts and Sciences, the American Association for the Advancement of Science, and the Econometric Society.

Ted Sanders is president of the Education Commission of the States. His wide experience in education includes serving as Southern Illinois University president, Ohio superintendent of public instruction, deputy U.S. secretary of education, Illinois state superintendent of education, and Nevada state superintendent of education. Besides having authored numerous articles, book chapters, guest editorials, and professional papers, he holds honorary doctorates from four institutions.

Philip Uri Treisman is a professor of mathematics and director of the Charles A. Dana Center for Mathematics and Science Education at the University of Texas. He serves as executive director of the Texas Statewide Systemic Initiative and leads a variety of state efforts focused on strengthening K-16 mathematics and science education. His research interests lie in education policy with a focus on the dynamics of education accountability and school finance systems.

Alexandra K. Wigdor is director of the National Research Council's Strategic Education Research Partnership. An NRC staff member since 1978, she most recently held the position of deputy director of the Commission on Behavioral and Social Sciences and Education with special responsibility for developing the education program. Among the notable reports on improving education produced that grew out of that program are *Improving Student Learning: A Strategic Plan for Education Research and Its Utilization* (1999); *Preventing Reading Difficulties in Young Children* (1998); *How People Learn: Mind, Brain, Experience, School* (1999); *How People Learn: Bridging Research and Practice* (1999); *Making Money Matter: Financing America's Schools* (1999), and *Eager to Learn: Educating Our Preschoolers* (2000).